Psychotherapy with "Impossible" Cases

The Efficient Treatment of Therapy Veterans

BY THE SAME AUTHORS

Escape from Babel:
Toward a Unifying Language for Psychotherapy Practice
Scott D. Miller, Barry L. Duncan, and Mark A. Hubble

Practical Solutions for School Problems: A Brief Intervention Approach
John J. Murphy and Barry L. Duncan

Handbook of Solution-Focused Brief Therapy:
Theory, Research, and Practice
Scott D. Miller, Mark A. Hubble, and Barry L. Duncan

The Miracle Method: A Radically New Approach to Problem Drinking
Scott D. Miller and Insoo Kim Berg

Finding the Adult Within: A Solution-Focused Self Help Guide
Barbara McFarland and Scott D. Miller

Changing the Rules: A Client-Directed Approach to Therapy
Barry L. Duncan, Andrew D. Solovey, and Gregory S. Rusk

Working with the Problem Drinker: A Solution-Focused Approach
Insoo Kim Berg and Scott D. Miller

Overcoming Relationship Impasses: Ways to Initiate Change When
Your Partner Won't Help
Barry L. Duncan and Joseph W. Rock

A NORTON PROFESSIONAL BOOK

Psychotherapy with "Impossible" Cases

The Efficient Treatment of Therapy Veterans

Barry L. Duncan
Nova Southeastern University
Ft. Lauderdale, Florida

Mark A. Hubble
Private Training and Consulting Practice
Upper Arlington, Ohio

Scott D. Miller
The Brief Therapy Training Consortium
Chicago, Illinois

W. W. Norton & Company
New York • London

Composition by Bytheway Typesetting Services, Inc.
Manufacturing by Haddon Craftsmen, Inc.

Library of Congress Cataloging-in-Publication Data

Duncan, Barry L.
    Psychotherapy with impossible cases : the efficient treatment of
therapy veterans / Barry L. Duncan, Mark A. Hubble, Scott D. Miller.
        p.   cm.
    Includes bibliographical references and index.
    ISBN 0-393-70246-4
    1. Impasse (Psychotherapy)   2. Psychotherapy—Failure.   3. Impasse
(Psychotherapy)—Case studies.   4. Psychotherapy—Failure—Case
studies.   5. Psychotherapy—Case studies.   I. Hubble, Mark A.,
1951–   .   II. Miller, Scott D.   III. Title.
RC489.I45D86   1997
616.89'14—dc20   96-35581   CIP

W. W. Norton & Company, Inc., 500 Fifth Avenue, New York, N. Y. 10110
http://www.wwnorton.com
W. W. Norton & Company, Ltd., 10 Coptic Street, London WC1A 1PU

1 2 3 4 5 6 7 8 9 0

To our parents,

Doris and Lee Duncan, Edith and John Hubble, and Darlene and
Paul Miller, for their loving "treatment" of their own
impossible cases

CONTENTS

PREFACE

In our clinical practice, with a frequency we would prefer neither to remember nor admit, we have met individuals who remained inured to our compassion, mired in their complaints, and unmoved by the profession's most sophisticated procedures and techniques. All therapists have had the experience of that sinking feeling in the pit of the stomach when certain names appear in their appointment books. Usually this uneasy sensation is not related to a dislike of the client or the clinician's malevolence, but rather to the therapist's experience of frustration and confusion because the case is not changing. That familiar feeling of dread is also connected to our ethics of responsibility and genuine sadness for the individual's plight in life. This mixture of compassion for the client, exasperation with treatment failure, and professional accountability can often blend to therapist burnout and an understandable resignation to the idea of "impossibility."

Impossible cases have always intrigued us. Eventually, we became curious about how impossibility comes about. We were no longer satisfied with answers that blamed the client or criticized the therapist. These explanations of impossibility kept us muddled and led nowhere. Consequently we decided to explore impossibility directly, through our own experience, so that we might discover ways to prevent, overcome, or circumvent it. We presented ourselves to the therapeutic and referral community as welcoming impossible cases. We offered free live-team consultation to therapists in the community who felt hopelessly stuck and wanted to bring their cases in search of new directions. In the provision of supervision and training, we invited live interviews with cases in which the individual therapist or agency was at an impasse with a client. Certain agencies regularly referred their "problem" cases to us. These cases were invariably multiple treatment failures and often were characterized by high risk of suicide, violence, abuse, or to many the worst risk, legal action.

Why did we accept such nightmarish cases? Are we crazy or arrogant, or both? While we may be a little crazy, we did not accept the cases because we thought we could cure them or offer something better (although we knew we could likely offer something different) than others before us. Rather, we intentionally took on these impossible cases because we believed then, and still do, that clients are the best teachers of psychotherapy. We believed that these cases could provide us with guidance where our chosen theories had fallen short. Clients who have not responded to therapy offered the best opportunity to learn about how impossibility develops and how the rules of impossibility could be changed. We learned far more from treatment failures than from those cases that seem charmed from beginning to end and/or confirmed our favorite theories. Essentially, we consulted with impossibility to gain new directions. This book is the product of that five-year consultation.

Previously we have said that our treatment failures taught us three conceptually simple, yet pragmatically difficult, lessons: (1) all theoretical models have limited applicability; (2) the therapeutic relationship is more valuable than expert interventions; and (3) what clients know, think, feel, and want has far more relevance to problem resolution than our favored academic conceptualizations (Duncan, Solovey, & Rusk, 1992). Our experiences with impossible cases have taught us yet another lesson: *Success can occur with impossibility when therapy is accommodated to the client's frame of reference and the client's theory of change is honored.* This book presents a practical application of that lesson.

In thinking about and working with impossibility, we searched for ways of understanding that helped us consider possibilities for positive outcomes. Because words are so important, we sought a description of seemingly intractable situations that would allow for an opportunity for success. We found the word "impracticable," which is defined by *Webster's Collegiate Dictionary* (1993) as "incapable of being accomplished by the means employed or at command." This word summarizes our view about impossibility. Clients and their predicaments are not impossible. Rather, they only seem so because of the impediments to success unwittingly imposed by a well-intended treatment process. When the "means employed" are changed from theory-directed to client-directed, then possibilities emerge. This book articulates how to conduct therapy under the client's direction.

Our view, of course, is not a mainstream perspective of psychotherapy, not to mention psychotherapy with cases that carry ominous diagnoses and seem impossible. You may look at the approach in this book in many ways. One is to see the notion of allowing the multiple treatment failure client to direct therapy as a creative, albeit unusual approach to use as a last resort once it appears obvious that more customary approaches have not been effective. Another way to understand this style of approaching difficult cases is that it represents a preferred method of treatment that permits inclusion of more traditional approaches as they are determined by clients to be helpful to their concerns. It is our hope that regardless of your theoretical preferences, you will experience, as we have, the delight and inspiration from observing clients considered impossible overcome seemingly insurmountable obstacles.

Psychotherapy with "Impossible" Cases is an explicit account of how to efficiently approach clients who have had negative experiences in therapy. While this book is devoted to the specifics of working with difficult cases, the approach rests on a conceptualization of psychotherapy that intentionally maximizes the known curative factors, as described more fully in *Escape From Babel: Toward A Unifying Language For Psychotherapy Practice* (Miller, Duncan, & Hubble, 1997). We view *"Impossible" Cases* as a companion work to *Escape From Babel*, but fully recognize that every work must stand on its own merit.

Any endeavor of this kind reflects contributions by many and to them we are deeply grateful. We are most indebted to our clients, who continue to inform and improve our work with their amazing resilience and incredulous abilities for change. Several people deserve special mention. In addition to the influences mentioned in our previous publications, we would like to acknowledge the inspiration provided by two parents of our field, Carl Rogers and John Weakland, who in retrospect attended different schools together. We hope that this book honors their memory. One of the authors (BD) is indebted to his early mentors, Steve McConnell, Russ Bent, and especially Scott Fraser. We owe a great debt of gratitude to our former colleagues at the Dayton Institute for Family Therapy. Paul Bruening taught us patience and the value of therapist restraint. Andy Solovey kept us grounded in social realities and connected to the client's desires. Finally Greg Rusk, one of the best therapists we have ever watched, predictably amazed us with his ability to be liked by clients from all walks of life.

We are grateful to Joe Rock, Rachel Merl, Paul Padlak, Jay McKeel, Annette Wilson, Martha Bouis, Jennifer Uustal, and Victoria Lichtman for critiquing the manuscript and strengthening its message. We are especially grateful to Shelley Lopez, John Murphy, and Justine Ritter, who contributed in many ways, far beyond the call of duty. Also, thanks to Chari and Larry Auerbach, Bob Peach, Estie Topfer, Aileen Erbacher, Dottie Moynihan, Wayne Galloway, Karen Reed, Jay Slayden, Joan Funk, Rebecca Ansted, and Linda Heinz for their comments, suggestions, and support. We are very grateful to Regina Dahlgren Ardini of Norton for skillful editorial help and her invariable cheerfulness. Finally, we feel especially indebted to Susan Barrows Munro at Norton for being there when we needed her the most.

Barry L. Duncan
Mark A. Hubble
Scott D. Miller

Psychotherapy with "Impossible" Cases

The Efficient Treatment of Therapy Veterans

EXPERIENTIAL AND EMPIRICAL INFLUENCES

If I can stop one heart from breaking,
I shall not live in vain;
If I can ease one life the aching,
Or cool one pain,
Or help one fainting robin
Unto his nest again,
I shall not live in vain.

Emily Dickinson

CHAPTER 1

Changing the Rules of Impossibility

Keep your hands open, and all the sands of the desert can pass through them. Close them, and all you can feel is a bit of grit.

Taisen Deshimaru

IMPOSSIBLE CASES MIGHT no longer be a luxury we can afford. As managed care companies proliferate, hardly any therapist can escape the "quality assurance" arm of their organizations. Quality assurance not only assesses the client's satisfaction with the services performed, it also aggressively monitors how well clinicians maintain cost-efficiency. Providers who return to the utilization management specialist, seeking authorization for more sessions or intensive treatment because of the perceived difficulty, complexity, and severity of their clients' problems are finding themselves without referrals. Or worse, they are being disinvited from provider panels. Undoubtedly, it is in everyone's interest—client, provider, third-party payer—to curtail and successfully manage impossibility in clinical practice.

In our five-year consultation with impossibility, we sought not to assign blame for intractable situations to therapists or clients, but to understand how impossibility developed so that a different journey could be charted by the client and therapist. We were most interested in the assumptions, attitudes, and actions inherent to psychotherapy itself that were the progenitors of impossibility. Our clients taught us four pathways that the therapeutic process unintentionally clears for unimpeded travel to treatment failure.

PATHWAYS TO IMPOSSIBILITY

What's in a Word?

A word carries far — very far — deals destruction through time as the bullets go flying through space.

Joseph Conrad

Historically, impossibility has been located in the client. Attributions of trait and character disturbance, ego compromise, or organically-sponsored deficit held the reins of clinical evaluations. A good example is found in the now common classification of borderline personality disorder. In one word, clinicians encounter a stereotype of trouble: predictable unpredictability, impulsiveness, dangerousness, unreasonableness, neediness, unmodulated emotional lability, dismal prognosis, and more. Faced with such an imposing array of symptoms and daunting characteristics, who would not feel a sinking sensation in the stomach and silently yearn for the Y.A.V.I.S (young, attractive, verbal, intelligent, and sensitive), cooperative client?

In this respect, one reliable pathway to the impossible case arises in the anticipation of impossibility. Whether the experience is borne in simple trait ascriptions or by establishing a formal diagnosis, once set in motion, the set or expectancy of hard going or poor outcome can be surprisingly resilient (Salovey & Turk, 1991). If left unchecked, the expectation becomes the person. In effect, the person is rendered "deindividuated," made equivalent to the characterization or label (Wright, 1991). Should this occur, observers (nonprofessionals and clinicians alike) will unwittingly distort information to conform with their expectations.

To illustrate, Temerlin (1968) produced a tape, later played to a study sample of psychiatrists, psychologists, and clinical psychology graduate students. The subjects were asked to decide whether the man in the tape was psychotic, neurotic, or healthy. Interestingly enough, the man was portrayed as successful in work, family and interpersonal relationships, and sexual intimacy. Confident and secure, with little competitiveness, arrogance, or grandiosity in his personality make-up, he reported having a rewarding childhood, good sense of humor, few anxieties about his life roles, and only reasonable worries. No pathologic symptoms were presented. In fact, he was the picture of a normal, healthy person.

In the first experimental condition, an eminent clinician introduced the tape by saying that the man shown was a "rare case of a mentally healthy individual." In the second condition, the same prestigious clinician suggested that the man "looks neurotic but is actually quite psychotic." Subjects in the third condition received no suggestion about the man's diagnostic status.

All the observers assessed the man as healthy in the first condition. In the one suggesting psychosis, 44% of the subjects evaluated the man as psychotic, 50% as neurotic, and 6% as healthy. In the final or control condition, 57% viewed him as healthy and 43% thought of him as neurotic. Further analysis found that in the psychosis condition, the inclination toward severe pathology was held most by the psychiatrists and least by the graduate students.

A more widely known experiment, published in *Science* in 1973, affirms the power of expectations. In this classic study, Rosenhan recruited and trained a group of normal confederates to obtain psychiatric hospitalization. To gain admission, they falsified a single psychotic symptom (hearing voices). The clinicians readily diagnosed the pretend patients as mentally ill (principally schizophrenic) and admitted them for stays ranging from 7 to 52 days. During their hospitalizations, the pseudopatients showed no sign of psychosis, yet the original diagnosis remained in place.

Rosenhan also demonstrated how the clinicians' initial expectations came to serve as confirmatory biases. In one instance, staff took truthful historical information provided by a pseudopatient and made it conform with prevailing theoretical notions about schizophrenia.

Specifically, a pretend patient told the staff that he had a close relationship with his mother, but was distant from his father during his early childhood. During his teenage years and beyond, he said he became very close with his father, while his relationship with his mother cooled. He characterized his relationship with his wife as close and warm and, except occasional arguments about everyday bothers, friction was minimal. He reported, too, that he was close to his children and very infrequently disciplined them by spanking.

In the following discharge summary, the staff's supposition about the meaning of the pseudopatient's self-report becomes apparent:

This white 39-year-old male . . . manifests a long history of considerable ambivalence in close relationships, which begins in early childhood. A warm relationship with his mother cools during his adolescence. A distant relationship to his father is described as becoming very intense. Affective stability is absent. His attempts to control emotionality with his wife and children are punctuated by angry outbursts and, in the case of the children, spankings. And while he says that he has several good friends, one senses considerable ambivalence embedded in those relationships also. (Rosenhan, 1973, p. 254)

The staff slanted the confederate's self-description to agree with a popular theory of schizophrenia. People with the diagnosis of schizophrenia are said to be strikingly ambivalent about their relationships. The inconsistency and vacillation in their feelings toward others are believed to surface in their commonplace, day-to-day thoughts. Yet, nothing approaching a psychotic level of ambivalence emerged in the pretend patient's reported relations with his parents, spouse, or friends. Where ambivalence could be inferred, it was probably no greater than the ebb and flow found in all human relationships. It is true the pseudopatient's relationship with his parents changed over time; even so, in the ordinary world that would be unremarkable.

Doubtless, the meaning assigned to his history (i.e., ambivalent feelings, emotional instability) was defined by the word *schizophrenia*. An entirely different meaning would presumably have been given if it were known that the man was "normal."

Despite our awareness of the many pitfalls of attribution effects, they continue to direct impression formation and undermine critical thinking. While we are conducting our professional routines and conversations, we may be concurrently transforming a case with potential into one with little if any at all. As the extant literature proves (Salovey & Turk, 1991), this process is robust, operates outside the range of awareness, and erodes the curative elements of therapy (Miller et al., 1997).

In outlining this pathway to impossibility, the intent is not to dismiss the benefits of accurate diagnoses, but to illustrate the dangers that can accompany the act of diagnosing and describing client problems.

We offer a pragmatic alternative to negative attribution effects that guides practice away from dismal prognoses.

Theory Countertransference

It is only theory that makes men completely incautious.
Bertrand Russell

Therapeutic traditions or conventions provide another pathway to impossibility. Traditions are important in all human pursuits, but they can also have inhibiting and damaging consequences. The source of psychotherapy's traditions are mainly grounded in theory, not fact, and yet they often assume the status of fact.

A clinician's loyalty to theoretical traditions and its later impact on the ways events are understood and handled in therapy is called "theory countertransference" (Hubble & O'Hanlon, 1992; O'Hanlon, 1990). Its role in the development of impossible cases is as powerful as diagnostic wording and language. In its more virulent form it causes theoretical fundamentalism and theory-driven political correctness.

In the strictest technical meaning, countertransference refers to an affective, largely unconscious process that takes place in the therapist and is triggered in relationship to the client. According to the classical psychoanalytic view, the nucleus of countertransference consists of the therapist's unresolved neurotic conflicts (Eisenbud, 1978). For a long time, it was believed to operate like emotional blinders. If unchecked, the psychoanalyst's countertransference was regarded as a real danger to the integrity of the treatment.

It is accepted in the psychodynamic tradition that the person of the therapist (the total of the clinician's responses, individual history, and state of mind) could be supportive or disruptive to the therapy. Less attention, however, was paid to how the therapist's overall conception of the human condition and therapy would affect treatment outcomes. When psychoanalysis was virtually the only psychotherapeutic approach available and was widely regarded as the truth, it was natural that its theoretical content and assumptions would not be questioned.

Despite the pressure that Freud placed on his followers to remain loyal to his doctrine, doubts and concern took root. Two of the first to call attention to the existence of theory countertransference (TC) were Salvador Ferenczi and Otto Rank, members of Freud's inner circle of followers. In 1925, they questioned certain tenets of the theoretical orthodoxy burgeoning in Freud's writing and recommended practice. The overall thrust of their critique was that psychoanalysts were elevating theory over therapy.

In particular, Ferenczi and Rank observed that in their eagerness to corroborate the theory with each patient, psychoanalysts frequently performed a complete psychoanalysis when it was not indicated. They described the unwelcome result of this practice as a prolonged and sterile treatment: rich in intellectualization, but bereft of emotional relevance (Flegenheimer, 1982). Ferenczi and Rank were criticizing how their colleagues placed more importance on proving the correctness of their theory than helping their analysands efficiently.

In the past thirty years, insight into the delimiting aspects of theoretical loyalty grew. For instance, Aldrich (1968) attacked the tendency of therapists to dismiss early improvement in treatment as a mere flight into health or transference cure. Underscoring the lack of evidence to support this and associated theoretical claims, he described how the insistence on their veracity amounted to a "pessimistic prediction." The effect on the client was to encourage dependency and a prolonged treatment promising "a long period of protection" (p. 41). He concluded that the benefits derived from treatment could evaporate in the hot house of theoretical bias, therapeutic perfectionism, and uncompromising use of techniques.

Milton Erickson pointedly spoke as well about the hazards of TC. For him, theoretical loyalty could lead to oversimplifications about people, close off possibilities for change, and promote technical inflexibility. His now famous quote summarizes his position on the role of theory in therapy:

Each person is an individual. Hence, psychotherapy should be formulated to meet the uniqueness of the individual's needs, rather than tailoring the person to fit the Procrustean bed of a hypothetical theory of human behavior. (Zeig & Gilligan, 1990, p. xix)

The proverbial story of the man who bought a hammer and then found that everything needed to be nailed suggests a broad effect of TC. Impossible cases may occur when the client hates the hammer, refuses to be nailed, and yet the blows continue. Clients hold their own theories about their psychology, difficulties, and life situation

(Duncan et al., 1992). When their points of view are ignored, dismissed, or trampled by the therapist's theory, noncompliance or resistance is a predictable outcome. To the therapist, the client begins to look, feel, and act impossible. To the client, the therapist comes across as uncaring, disinterested, or patently wrong. At this stage, the therapy has changed from a helping relationship to a clash of cultures with no one the winner.

This is not to suggest that theory is the root of all evil. Yet, theory is often overapplied and the benefits of allegiance are overstated. This book demystifies theoretical models as potentially helpful lenses to be shared with deference to their fit to the client's "frame" and prescription. Here they are regarded as lenses to try, each with its own characteristic style, shade, and correction, permitting the richness and diversity of different approaches to remain intact as well as protecting the therapist from TC.

This book presents a method for redirecting therapy from confirming theory-driven objective truths to discovering subjective truths that promote possibilities for change by the client.

Doing More of the Same

The more things change, the more they remain the same.
Alfonse Karr

TC fosters impossibility by (a) pursuing agendas applicable to the clinicians' theoretical premises and (b) violating the client's sensibilities and beliefs. Similarly, impossible cases arise by persisting in a therapeutic approach that is not working. Perhaps more than any others, the group of researchers and clinicians comprising the Mental Research Institute (MRI) have examined this pathway to impossibility.

In several works, including *Change: Problem Formation and Problem Resolution* (Watzlawick, Weakland, & Fisch, 1974), the MRI sought to determine how problems begin and persist. They reasoned that stubborn or unmanageable problems, those that are often called chronic, cannot be sufficiently explained on the basis of some innate characteristic of the client. Rather, they concluded that the unyielding or impossible nature of a problem arises in the very efforts to solve it.

The MRI sees problems beginning in some ordinary difficulty, of which there are no shortage in our lives. Most difficulties create discomfort and during these challenging times people will employ the strategies that have helped before. Ordinarily, the tried and true solutions work, but sometimes they fall short.

According to the MRI, for a difficulty to turn into a problem, only two conditions need be fulfilled. First, the difficulty is mishandled (the attempted solution doesn't work). And second, when the difficulty proves refractory, more of the same ineffective solution is applied. What happens then is that the original difficulty will deteriorate. Over time, a vicious, downwardly spiraling cycle ensues with the original difficulty growing into an impasse, immense in size and importance (Weakland, Fisch, Watzlawick, & Bodin, 1974).

The problem, once perceived as a problem, embraces not only the original dilemma, but also all the failed, repetitive efforts to find resolution. The cycle of problem expression followed by failed solutions is surprisingly vigorous. It occurs despite the best intentions of those involved, and the participants' recognition that the attempts at solution are inadequate. The solution has become the impossible problem.

Therapists are no stranger to the complaint-solution cycle just described. Intractability and impossibility develop in clinical situations when therapists repeatedly apply the same or similar therapeutic strategy. This process can start in a surprisingly short period. Therapists "doing more of the same" are convinced that persistence will win the day, even when all the evidence suggests that the strategy is ineffectual. The rationale for applying the same solution can be as simple as, "If at first you don't succeed, then try, try again," to the most elaborate theoretical system. Yet, regardless of the differing inducements and explanations, the result is equivalent.

All theoretical models and therapeutic strategies are inherently limited and will generate their share of impossibility when repetitively applied. So far, the response to this problem has been characterized by the development of different schools of psychotherapy, each supposedly corrected for the inadequacies of the others. Over 400 rival approaches have emerged that in many ways seem little more than packaged products competing for their share of the marketplace.

The whole notion of developing more models to solve the problem of impossibility is an excellent example of "doing more of the same." In this book, we invite you to consider something quite different. We do not advocate a new theoretical frame of reference to guide your practice. Instead, we offer practical methods of taking the approach for therapy from the client's world view.

What's the Motivation?

Beware lest you lose the substance by grasping at the shadow.
Aesop

An additional pathway to impossibility is created when one neglects the client's motivation. There is no such individual as an unmotivated client. Clients may not, as we have found all too often, share ours, but they certainly hold strong motivations of their own. An unproductive and futile therapy can come about by mistaking or overlooking what the client wants to accomplish, misapprehending the client's readiness for change, or pursuing a personal motivation.

Research has now established that the critical process-outcome link in successful therapy is the quality of the client's participation (Orlinsky, Grawe, & Parks, 1994). Clients who collaborate in therapy, are engaged with the therapist, and involve themselves with a receptive and open mind will likely profit. Owing to the importance of clients' positive involvement for outcome, their motivation—not only just for being in therapy, but also for achieving their own goals—has to be understood, respected, and actively incorporated into the treatment. To do less or to impose agendas motivated by theoretical prerogatives, personal bias, and perhaps some sense of what would be good for the client, invites impossibility.

Before leaving the role of motivation in impossible cases, the place of "saving face" should be considered. When clients feel overwhelmed and stuck, they are apt to experience their problems as impossible. Seeking help offers the prospect of something better. Simultaneously, it may also signify their failure to resolve the problem on their own. In fact, their feelings of failure may be so acute that they crowd out any favorable self-evaluation. In these circumstances, going to therapy can represent just one more unpleasant reminder of how badly they have managed their difficulties. Humiliation is added to insult.

If a therapist then suggests or implies that the client's point of view is wrong, somehow invalidate, or upstage the client, "resistance" may appear. After all, even if not already demoralized, who wants to be reminded of failure, criticized, judged, or made to feel that you have to follow orders? What we come to call resistance may sometimes reflect the client's attempt to salvage a small portion of self-respect. As such, some cases become impossible simply because the treatment allows the client no way of "saving face" or upholding dignity. This is probably what Milton Erickson had in mind when he suggested that the art of therapy revolves around helping clients to bow out of their symptoms gracefully. He recognized that clients simultaneously hold a desire to change and a natural tendency to protect themselves if change (for worse or for better) compromises personal dignity.

This book offers ways of circumventing impossibility created by inattention to motivation. We illustrate a clinical style that embraces client motivations and proactively preserves client dignity through each phase of treatment.

MOLLY: AN IMPOSSIBLE CASE IN POINT

In one of our more recent cases the pathways to impossibility converged. The intersection of what we call "attribution creep," theory countertransference, doing more of the same, and inattention to motivation made for an unremitting predicament.

Molly, a delightful and precocious 10-year-old, was originally referred for treatment by her mother. Molly's parents were divorced. She was sleeping in mother's bed and having trouble adjusting to a new apartment, school, and friends. In an intake performed at their HMO clinic, Molly was identified as coming from a "dysfunctional family." She also was described as being "triangulated" in parental conflict. Diagnosed as having "separation anxiety disorder," she was referred to a weekly children's social skills group.

After a few weeks in group, mother reported that Molly was experiencing nightmares. The group therapist responded by also seeing Molly individually. For her treatment, the following goals were established: (1) increase Molly's understanding of being in control of her behavior and increase responsible behavior, (2) relieve her fears about moving and adjusting to a new school and friends, (3) remove Molly from parental conflict, and (4) help Molly return to her own room to sleep.

The therapist pursued Molly's impressions of her parent's relationship and encouraged her to remove herself from their problems. Following six months of concurrent group and individual treatment, there was little improvement. Thinking this step might help, Molly's mother next requested a female therapist.

Mother's wishes were respected and a female therapist assumed the girl's care. Because Molly asked if her therapist ever felt ugly, it was surmised that Molly had self-esteem issues. Individual therapy now revolved around playing games to see what "themes came out." The therapist also suspected sexual abuse. Her goals for Molly's treatment were: (1) explore for sexual abuse, and (2) investigate Molly's feelings about her father.

Still concerned about her daughter's lack of progress, mother requested authorization for a therapist outside the clinic. The authorization committee met and decided that a psychiatric evaluation was in order. The psychiatric evaluation noted that Molly still slept in mother's room and that somatic complaints and school avoidance remained. Imipramine was prescribed to relieve Molly's separation anxiety. No change occurred in her condition.

Molly, in twice-weekly treatment for over a year and now on medication, had become, at the age of 10, an impossible case. Looking back, we can reconstruct how customary practice contributed to the evolution of impossibility.

A cautionary note is warranted before proceeding. In any retrospective analysis of impossibility, it is tempting to create straw men. If only the therapists were smarter, more astute, or "theoretically correct" then the impossible case would have never evolved. Likewise, if the client was more open-minded, compliant, or healthy, then a good outcome would be assured. These assertions are useless. "Shoot the therapist" or "shoot the client" are misdirected pastimes. *The real culprits are the pathways to impossibility themselves.* These processes, borne in our training, traditions, and practice, can get the best of any of us. We all fall victim to them. So then how did they operate in Molly's case?

First, attribution creep influenced her therapy. The explanatory labels colored how Molly was regarded by her helpers. She became a psychological/psychiatric condition, a phenomenon observed in Rosenhan's (1973) research. For instance, when she asked her individual therapist about having ever felt ugly, Molly's question was assumed to be symptomatic of self-esteem issues. The possibility that her question reflected natural curiosity or the normal concerns of a preadolescent was not or perhaps could not be entertained. Because the categories of "dysfunctional family," "triangulated," and a "separation anxiety disorder" were established, her treaters were constrained to perceive her behavior through the perceptual filters created by the diagnoses and clinical descriptions.

Second, theory countertransference took hold. Molly's first therapist, perhaps following a family therapy tradition, investigated the relationship between Molly's symptoms and her parent's conflict. The therapist followed this line of inquiry despite an unremitting problem and mother's view that triangulation was not relevant. In addition, from the outset of her treatment, there was no evidence to suggest that Molly was a victim of sexual abuse. Throughout all her therapies, sexual victimization was never brought up by Molly or her mother, or confirmed. Yet, because it was hypothesized by one of her therapists, a goal was set to explore for it. The therapy then was sidetracked from directly resolving the presenting complaint toward satisfying the requirements of a theory. This was not an agenda shared with the client or her mother.

Third, doing more of the same was in force. Each therapy persisted in a chosen approach (de-triangulation, exploration for abuse, social skills training, medication) in the face of direct evidence that the problem was not changing. Although on the face of it, the therapies looked different (group, individual, psychopharmacotherapy), they operated on the shared view that Molly suffered from a disorder and something could be done to her that would alleviate the problem. Additionally, doing more of the same was found in the therapists' assumption of an expert role. The helpers met, assessed Molly, assigned both the diagnoses and the interventions. She was left out of the decision making but was expected to participate.

This latter point bears on the fourth pathway to impossibility, inattention to the client's motivation. The goals and tasks selected for Molly's treatment did not reflect her input. The clinicians apparently omitted asking Molly for her ideas about her problem or possible solutions. What she thought or wanted wielded little influence in their deliberations. We later learned that Molly "resisted" her therapists' efforts to change her. She felt she was not allowed to preserve her pride; to comply incurred too much loss of face. We will revisit Molly in Chapter 2.

Once again, after impossibility develops, it is tempting to criticize the therapists. If only they had taken this tack or pursued this avenue, then everything would have turned out well and impossibility would have been averted. Because the pathways we have described are so easy to follow, borne out too many times in our own experience with clients, this book will focus on what to do to prevent the evolution of impossibility or correct it.

EFFICIENT TREATMENT

The current zeitgeist for efficiency is best reflected in the now bursting at the seams *brief therapy* literature. The data are difficult to ignore: the comparable outcome of short- versus long-term therapy, client expectations that therapy will last 6–10 sessions, and the largest proportion of change in therapy occurring in 6–8 sessions (Budman & Gurman, 1988; Koss & Shiang, 1994). For us, brief therapy highlights the value of efficiency in clinical practice, achieving a successful outcome in the fewest sessions possible.

Brief Versus Efficient

Although "brief" is currently in vogue, we prefer to work in the context of the word "efficient" for three reasons. First, one of the primary claims made about brief therapy is that it is, in fact, briefer. Advocates within the brief therapy movement assert that their approaches help clients spend less time resolving difficulties than other, traditional, "non-brief" approaches. With regard to the duration of treatment, however, the research literature shows rather convincingly that all therapy is relatively brief in duration. Indeed, data collected over the last fifty years consistently shows that the average client attends only a handful of sessions regardless of the treatment model employed (Garfield, 1978; Koss & Butcher, 1986; Miller,

1994). In one particularly telling example, Garfield (1989) investigated the length of treatment for clinicians practicing long-term, psychodynamic psychotherapy at the Veterans' Administration in 1949 and found that the average client attended only 6 sessions.

Therapy simply is, for the most part, brief *regardless of the treatment model employed*. "Brief," therefore, says nothing about effectiveness and speaks only to the time spent in treatment, which is virtually a shared phenomenon among all approaches. Efficient therapy is characterized by both brevity and effectiveness.

Second, "brief" is often used to rationalize an a priori fixed number of sessions determined by the therapist or setting in which he or she works. Interestingly, when brief therapists attempt to set limits on the number of sessions a client may attend in advance, that treatment is typically longer than therapies in which no time limits are set (Orlinsky et al., 1994). While we are aligned with the values of brief therapy, we are more committed to the ideal of pursuing a successful outcome, as defined by the client, in the fewest possible sessions. This may occur in two sessions or twenty. Efficient therapy, we believe, occurs as a natural consequence of accepting the client's frame of reference as the guiding theory for intervention.

Finally, "brief" is often interpreted as "bandaid" therapy or as not really addressing issues of depth. As the accomplishments of our clients will illustrate, time in efficient treatment has little correlation with the depth or breadth of client achievement.

Effectiveness

While the brief therapy research literature sings the praises of shorter-term approaches, the outcome literature speaks directly to the effectiveness of treatment, the actual contributions to success in therapy. A review of the outcome literature (Lambert, Shapiro, & Bergin, 1986; Miller et al., 1997), as depicted in the figure, suggests that 30% of observed change is accounted for by the common (relationship) factors. Common factors are the similarities found across therapies regardless of theoretical orientation. Techniques, or those aspects that are specific to a particular orientation, are responsible for 15% of positive outcome, as are expectancy/placebo effects (improvement resulting from the client's knowledge of being in treat-

Change in Therapy

Factors Influencing Successful Outcome*

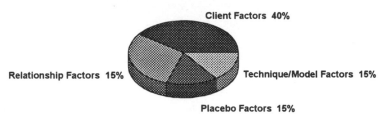

Client Factors 40%

Relationship Factors 15%

Technique/Model Factors 15%

Placebo Factors 15%

*Data from Lambert, 1992

ment). Accounting for the remaining 40% of successful outcome are the extratherapeutic (client) variables, or the factors that are part of the client and his or her environment that contribute to change *regardless* of the client's participation in therapy (Lambert, 1992).

Although it was initially troubling to recognize that effectiveness had little to do with theoretical cleverness or technical wizardry, we finally embraced the data that place the client's contribution to successful outcome as most significant, followed by the common factors (Miller et al., 1997). Our favorite theories proved to be far less significant to the change process than we have all been led to believe. One cynical conclusion that perhaps can be drawn from the empirical suggestion that therapy models are only modestly influential to positive outcome, is that good marketing can overcome bad data. Marketing hype about new, improved, or different techniques unfortunately obscures what already exists that is far more consequential to how people change in therapy (Miller et al., 1996).

The value of brevity and the desire for effectiveness combined in our pursuit of efficiency of treatment. Efficient therapy de-emphasizes, but does not eliminate, theory in service of highlighting the client's perspective, actively applies outcome research and the known curative factors, and maximizes the client's participation through all phases of treatment.

THE CLIENT AS A VETERAN

While working with impossible cases and treatment failures can invoke many descriptors, and usually does just that, we prefer to refer to individuals who have been involved in therapy and for whatever reason have not succeeded as *veterans*. They are veterans of a struggle for a better life. They show the wear and tear of their battles with change in various forms, ranging from hopelessness about, to hostility toward treatment. Unfortunately, these veterans of misery have often been kicked around by the mental health system and perceive therapists as discounting their desires, discrediting their distress, and even disbelieving their stories of misfortune. Like many veterans, they are battle weary, very cautious, and a little crusty around the edges. Also like many veterans, they have their stories to tell.

This book is about their stories of tragedy and triumph. They are the main characters in their real-life dramas, not us, not therapists. We are cast only in supportive roles. This book does not spin yarn after yarn of clinical conquest that relies on the theoretical savvy or technical expertness of the therapist; it will not make you a clever therapist in that sense.

De Shazer cogently describes the unfortunate tendency to glorify the therapist's input to success while excluding the client's in a comparison between accounts of Erickson's magical successes and the fictional powers of Sherlock Holmes:

It then dawned on me that Erickson-the-clever stories, like the Sherlock Holmes stories, actually under-develop or under-realize all the other characters that appear in the stories, particularly the clients. Sometimes these other characters, like Inspector Lestrade, no matter how important to the story itself, are just cardboard cutouts. We have little or no idea about their contributions to the therapeutic endeavor. . . . clever therapy depends on having clients and therapists cleverly working together in clever ways. (1994, pp. 33–34)

In service of keeping the client's story of success central to this book, we will, whenever possible, insert the client's own words, including his or her evaluation of what was helpful. It is one of our explicit goals to respect and illustrate the client's contribution to successful outcome.

The veterans whose treatments are depicted in this book warrant some additional comments and qualifying remarks. All of the cases in this book were diagnosed by previous providers, which we accepted at face value. Our work with these veterans focused on finding new directions and therefore did not include any heavy emphasis on differential diagnostics. While one may justifiably criticize the diagnostic acumen of those clinicians, the cases, nevertheless, invariably represent the failure of the therapeutic process as well as the exasperation of previous providers.

All of the cases in this book are real. Only names and identifying information have been altered to protect client confidentiality. The excerpted dialogues are from verbatim transcripts taken from videotaped sessions. They have only been edited and condensed for space and clarity; the clients' and therapists' words have not been changed.

The excerpts illustrate the points and issues raised in this book, but are not intended to represent *all* of what happened in treatment. Experienced clinicians know that therapy is not always stimulating or insightful, and does not invariably invoke images of brass bands and fireworks. We do not intend to present it as such. What is presented did occur, but other things occurred as well, such as irrelevant conversations, questions and comments by the therapist that led nowhere, and discussions that can only be described as uneventful.

Finally, if the cases seem to fit our approach perfectly, they do. They fit so well because our style and method emerged from these cases; our clinical experience informed our approach, not vice-versa.

CHANGING THE RULES: FROM IMPOSSIBILITY TO IMPRACTICABILITY

We would like you to consider treating veterans by allowing their frame of reference to guide your actions. Within the client is a theory of change waiting for discovery, a framework for intervention to be unfolded and intentionally accommodated for a successful outcome. Each client presents the therapist with a new theory to learn, a new language to practice, and new intervention applications to suggest. Psychotherapy, then, is an unique synthesis of ideas that evolves a new theory with explanatory and predictive validity for the client's specific circumstance. This book illustrates how to learn the client's theory of change, and accommodate therapy to that theory as a pathway out of impossibility. We believe that such a direction changes impossible situations into impracticable ones.

In asserting this client-directed style of addressing impossibility in treatment, we are not condemning theory or attempting to cast disparaging remarks at approaches that posit particular methods of treatment of difficult cases. These approaches have established their value and found a place in the repertoire of the informed clinician. Recall that it is our assertion that it is not the theory, the therapist, or the client that creates impossibility, but rather the pathways themselves that require circumvention. It is not our intent to set up adversaries to bolster our approach at the expense of a biased and oversimplistic criticism of more theory-driven approaches. It is our intent, however, to contrast a more traditional theory- directed point of view with the approach presented in this book. Readers may then draw their own conclusions about the advantages and pitfalls of both approaches.

ORGANIZATION OF THIS BOOK

This book attempts to turn up the heat on the unconventional idea of taking the client's frame of reference as an actual theory of change to be learned and intentionally applied to construct the best possible chance for a positive outcome. We believed that our point of view would be imminently more interesting and influential if we used as illustrations those cases that cause many clinicians either to shudder in fear or to consider hopeless when confronted in treatment. However, impossibility is not a prerequisite for considering the client's world view as superior to the therapist's. A compelling empirical argument is made in Chapter 2 for a proactive therapeutic approach that de-emphasizes theory and seeks deliberate enhancement of the powerful forces for change contained in the client's perception of a strong alliance. Chapter 2 also defines *accommodation* as the central style of this approach. Chapter 3 presents the general principles of working with those cases that send chills down our spines and provides sound pragmatic steps for avoiding the pathways identified in Chapter 1. Chapters 4 and 5 describe a practical format for approaching impossibility and detail the specific methodology for elevating the client's frame to a position of directing therapeutic choices. In the chapters that follow, a remarkable company of veterans will be introduced. Chapters 6, 7, and 8 present three impossible cases (dissociative identity [multiple personality] disorder, delusional [paranoia] disorder, and borderline personality disorder). To provide the reader with an alternative valid point of view, each case example chapter briefly surveys the prevailing convention regarding the diagnosis under scrutiny and the suggested course of treatment. The case is then presented in contrast. Chapter 9 summarizes our main points through a presentation of the "failed case" that taught us the most about impossibility. Chapter 9 concludes our discussion with our evaluation of theory- versus client-directed approaches.

CHAPTER 2

Accommodating Therapy to the Client's Frame of Reference: The Empirical Argument

Until lions have their historians, tales of hunting will always glorify the hunter.

African proverb

AS CLINICIANS, WE ARE REGULARLY BOMBARDED with what's new and different by workshop and conference brochures, book announcements, and other marketing devices aimed at our continuing education moneys. Most, if not all of what is sold is theory driven, technique oriented, or features a "master" therapist. This is not a criticism. Rather, it is an observation that what is most often highlighted is the therapist's frame of reference about psychotherapy. This is a curious phenomenon given the now strong evidence that other aspects of the psychotherapeutic process are far more influential in determining success in therapy (Miller et al., 1997).

This chapter will highlight a different point of view—namely the client's. An empirical argument evolving from 40 years of outcome research, as well as recent findings addressing the client's perception of the therapeutic alliance, is presented. The empirical literature challenges an emphasis on theoretical frames of reference and offers a persuasive argument to allow the client to direct the therapeutic process (Duncan & Moynihan, 1994). This chapter proposes that therapists intentionally accommodate therapy to the client's frame of reference for the explicit purpose of influencing successful outcome.

Our discussion begins by defining two central terms: accommodate and frame of reference.

ACCOMMODATING THE CLIENT'S FRAME OF REFERENCE

Definitions

Webster's Collegiate Dictionary (1993) defines *accommodate* as: (1) to make fit, suitable, or congruous; (2) to bring into agreement or concord; (3) to provide with something desired, needed, or suited; (4) a. to make room for, b. to hold without crowding or inconvenience, to contain comfortably; (5) to give consideration to, allow for; (6) to adapt oneself.

Accommodation (the act of accommodating) involves the therapeutic process of:

- making room for the client's resources and views.
- providing the conditions for change.
- responding with flexibility.
- adapting or making therapy fit the client's ideas of what is helpful.
- identifying the client as the most important part of the change process.

The client, then, is like a welcomed guest in your house of therapy. You are the gracious host doing everything possible to ensure that your guest is comfortable, that his or her special needs are met, that his or her views are respected, and that the visit is experienced as positive. Just as the host accommodates the guest, the therapist places the highest premium on the client's frame of reference.

The client's *frame of reference* is characterized by the client's (1) resources, skills, and abilities to solve the presenting problem in and out of therapy; (2) perceptions and experience of the therapeutic relationship; and (3) perceptions and experience of the presenting complaint, its causes, and how therapy may best address the client's goal. We call the latter the client's theory of change.

ACCOMMODATING THE CLIENT'S RESOURCES

Recall that extratherapeutic or client factors account for 40% of success in therapy. Client factors include the client's strengths, innate capacities for growth, and abilities to secure and make use of support and help from others. Also included are fortuitous or chance events that occur outside of therapy that clients may seize as opportunities for change. Client factors are foremost in significance to successful outcome, regardless of the therapist's theoretical orientation or the client's diagnosis.

Intervention at its best creates a context for the client's resources to be expressed. Accommodating client resources means highlighting client strengths and abilities rather than deficits and liabilities. Part of highlighting client strengths translates to discovering the client's answer or solution to the situation that precipitated therapy.

Molly* was introduced in the first chapter. She is a 10-year-old suffering from nightmares and an inability to sleep in her own room. Before a referral to us, Molly saw two therapists, was in both individual and group therapy, and had been prescribed an antidepressant. Molly traveled all four paths to impossibility.

Molly provides a strong endorsement to the empirical data that indicate the dramatic importance of the client and what he or she already possesses. Her case also illustrates that efficiency with impossible cases requires the therapist to allow the client's resources and solutions to take center stage. In the first session with Molly, we asked her what she believed would be helpful for resolving the "nightmares and sleeping in her room" problem. To this, Molly expressed astonishment that someone finally wanted her opinion. She then suggested she could barricade herself in her bed with pillows and stuffed animals.

In session two, she reported her plan was working, and therapy ended shortly after. As Molly illustrates, efficient treatment involves eliciting from the client those strengths, resources, and positive attributes that are needed to resolve the presenting problem. The therapist makes room for and gives utmost consideration to what the client brings as the most salient factor in achieving the desired outcome.

---

*The case of Molly has generated its share of controversy. Those who have viewed the videotape in workshops have overwhelmingly been charmed by Molly's spunk and insightfulness, and delighted at her incisive characterization of her previous therapies and what is helpful about therapy. However, some reviewers who read the case prior to publication have strongly criticized it as unrepresentative, naive, and simplistic. Molly's simple solution to her problem was perhaps too much of a non sequitor to the presumed complexity of this case, leading some to discount the outcome. This is precisely our point regarding the inherent obstacles that the helping process itself imposes on cases that do not respond to traditional intervention. When the pathways are circumvented, sometimes the solution *is* simple. One prominent reviewer was offended by our "joining with the girl as if she were unquestionably telling the absolute truth," was "embarrassed" by our "complete induction into her view," and criticized us because we "fell in love with her." We are guilty as charged on all three counts—except we see these criticisms as major strengths in approaching impossible cases.

Accommodate Versus Utilize

We prefer the connotation of the word "accommodate" over the word "utilize." Milton Erickson first used the term utilization as a way of "exploring a patient's individuality to ascertain what life learnings, experiences, and mental skills are available to deal with the problem [and] then utilize[ing] these uniquely personal internal responses to achieve therapeutic goals" (Erickson & Rossi, 1979, p. 1). Perhaps we are overly sensitive to the view of psychotherapy that promotes the therapist's technical expertise as the cause of therapeutic success, but utilization seems to highlight the therapist's skill in using the client's abilities rather than the client's abilities themselves. We favor the view that therapy creates a space for clients to employ their strengths to achieve their therapeutic goals and therapists are resources that *clients* utilize in their self-change process (Bohart & Tallman, 1996; Greening, 1996).

Molly: Making the Impossible Simple

The excerpts that follow come from session three. They reflect Molly's unsolicited observations about what was helpful and not helpful in her treatment experiences.

T: Well, how is it going?

M: Just fine. I'm sleeping in my own room. I've been in my own room since I've told you about it.

T: That's great! That's wonderful! I'm impressed by that still.

M: Psychiatrists [therapists] just don't understand . . . you [the client] also have the solutions, for yourself, but they say, "Let's try this and let's try that" and they're not helping. You know, you're like, "I don't really want to do that." Your asking me what I wanted to do with my room, got me back in my room. *So, what I'm saying to all psychiatrists is we have the answers, we just need someone to help us bring them to the front of our head.* It's like they're [the solutions] locked in an attic or something. It's a lot better when you ask a person what they want to do and they usually tell you what they think would help, but didn't know if it was going to help and didn't want to try.

She repeatedly recommends that clients be asked about their ideas, then make suggestions as fitting. Molly now speaks to what it was like for her to find her own solution to the sleeping problem.

M: I feel a lot better now that I came up with the solution to sleep in my own room and I did it and I'm proud of myself. And I couldn't be proud of myself if you told me, "How about if you barricade yourself in with pillows, maybe that'll work." I wouldn't feel like I've done it, so basically what I'm saying is, *you don't get as much joy out of doing something when somebody told you to do it; you want to be proud of it.*

Molly derived her own solution and it enhanced her self-esteem. When provided the opportunity, Molly revealed her inventiveness. When given the space, her resources became apparent. Her "pillow barricade" worked and she continued to sleep in her room without nightmares. Her other complaints also resolved in short order.

In Molly's case, as soon as her resources and ideas were allowed central consideration, when she was regarded as a competent partner in her own treatment by inviting her solutions, her sleep disturbance ended. We present her situation not to condemn the previous therapists, to suggest we hold magical solutions, or imply that all therapies will be similar. Instead, we see her story as a good example of client resources and their accommodation.

In addition to asking clients directly about their ideas, client resources can also be highlighted by inquiring about pretreatment changes and exceptions to the problem. We will discuss these avenues of accommodating client resources and ideas in Chapter 4. Client abilities are the most powerful resource, by far, that a therapist has.

ACCOMMODATING THE THERAPEUTIC RELATIONSHIP

Relationship (common) factors have been conceptualized in a variety of ways. Lambert and Bergin (1994) include empathy, warmth, acceptance, and encouragement of risk taking. They suggest that *most* of the success gained from intervention can be attributed to these factors. Clients consistently attribute their success to the relationship. That these qualities bear a striking resemblance to each other across studies is not coincidental. The quality of the relationship is a central contributor to therapeutic progress. Its significance transcends the most respected models and research-validated techniques.

Recall that the common factors contribute 30% of successful outcome, while technique/specific orientation account for only 15% of the variance. The outcome literature dispels the notion that any theoretical approach contains inherent or invariant validity and looms large over holding the therapist's theoretical view in any position of authority over the client.

Also challenging devotion to a chosen model and illuminating the importance of the relationship is the *equivalence of outcome* finding. Despite Herculean efforts by loyal followers, there has been no demonstrated superiority of one approach over another. The equivalence of outcome finding has been documented in several reviews (Bergin & Lambert, 1978; Luborsky, Singer, & Luborsky, 1975; Orlinsky & Howard, 1986; Sloane, Staples, Cristol, Yorkston, & Whipple, 1975; Smith, Glass, & Miller, 1980), and more recently in the NIMH multisite study of depression (Elkin et al., 1989). The failure to find differential outcomes in studies comparing therapies that use highly divergent techniques supports the importance of common factors to positive outcome (Arkowitz, 1992; Lambert, 1992), and casts serious doubt on pledging allegiance to any approach.

Yet another empirical affront to the therapist's frame of reference is provided by research demonstrating that client, not therapist, perceptions of the relationship are the *most* consistent predictor of improvement (Gurman, 1977; Horowitz, Marmar, Weiss, DeWitt, & Rosenbaum, 1984; Lafferty, Beutler, & Crago, 1989). More recently the relationship has been studied in terms of the therapeutic *alliance*, which includes both therapist and client contributions, and emphasizes collaboration in achieving the goals of therapy (Marmar, Horowitz, Weiss, & Marziali, 1986).

Accentuating many previous findings regarding client perceptions of the relationship, Bachelor (1991) found that client perceptions of the alliance yield stronger predictions of outcome than therapists', and that from the client's view, the most salient factors to success are therapist-provided warmth, help, caring, emotional involvement, and efforts to explore relevant (to the client) material.

Consider Molly's following statements in light of the significance of client perceptions of the relationship/alliance to positive outcome. In this passage, she comments on having her ideas neglected.

M: My other therapists never asked me what I wanted to work on. They asked me questions about the subjects that I don't really want to answer. Shouldn't I be telling you [therapist] what I think about this?

T: [Laughs]

M: I mean you're not here to tell me my life or anything. I should come in and tell the person, "This is what's happening with this situation" and they're [the therapists] saying "Your mom tells me you're doing such and such a thing" and then there's more stuff and like, *when did I start having problems with that?* [therapist laughs] And you come in there to talk to a person, to get them [problems] out of your system and get them worked on. Instead of she [the therapist] telling or he telling you what he thinks has happened, "Your Dad's doing this, your grandfather's doing this," it's not really helping because you're sitting there going, "Uh-huh, uh-huh" and that's why I usually dreaded going to therapy. It never worked, it never helped. She [the therapist] sat down, and she starts talking. I'm sitting there going [demonstrates her posture, looking down] she talked the whole hour and I barely got a sentence in!

T: Certainly that wasn't very helpful to your concerns, your sleeping in your own room.

M: She ignored me being in Mom's room. . . . And it is like they [therapists] think they are some almighty power or something! [Both laugh]

T: That drives me nuts about therapists when they think they are the almighty word about things.

M: Like they are God. [Molly sings as if in a choir]

T: Right [laughs]. Oh that is music to my ears, Molly! You know, we think a lot alike.

M: It's like hang on, *I am also somebody.* And you, you laugh at what I mean to be funny, and back at my old therapist whenever I said something, well I tried to say something about a subject, she gets busted up. It's like, hey I have an opinion too!

T: She did not take you seriously.

M: No!

In reviewing the above transcripted dialogue, recall that this is the same child placed in a social skills group, and treated individually for over a year! We say this not to criticize her previous therapists, but rather to emphasize how compelling the pathways to impossibility really are.

Molly makes it clear she felt discounted and ignored. What she perceived as important and what she valued were not solicited. Given the significance of the client's perceptions of the relationship and the quality of the client's participation in therapy, it is not difficult to see why Molly did not have a successful treatment experience. While Molly's opinions were perhaps ignored because of her age, we believe that adults are often similarly discounted.

Accommodating the therapeutic relationship means containing the client comfortably, providing for the client's desires, and making the relationship fit the client's perceptions of empathy, warmth, etc. (Miller et al., 1997). Accommodation emphasizes therapist monitoring of the client's response to the process itself and quickly adjusting as necessary to calibrate therapy to the client's expectations. For example, in a study examining client perceptions of empathy, Bachelor (1988) found that 44% of clients perceived their therapist's empathy as cognitive, 30% as affective, 18% as sharing, and 7% as nurturant. Empathy has different meanings to different clients and therapists must accommodate their approach to the client's view of a helpful relationship.

The Case of Barb

Forty years of research indicate that the client's perceptions of the therapeutic process are important to successful outcome. Relationship factors and client perceptions of therapist behaviors, however, may not be viewed as exciting as the latest line of techniques, and consequently are often overlooked. Consider Barb's story.

Barb was diagnosed borderline and sent to us because she complained about two therapists and requested an outside of agency referral. Barb's story was a gut-wrenching tragedy. Her history included a childhood experience of a terrible accident that killed both her father and her sister, multiple incidents of sexual abuse, and growing up without a parent because of her mother's total collapse after the accident. Barb was taking antidepressants, often hospitalized for suicidal behavior, and frequently called her therapist. Previous therapists dealt with this situation by setting limits and becoming frustrated.

The new therapist responded to the calls, allowing the relationship to unfold and the alliance to develop. Running counter to the often-given advice about establishing boundaries with borderlines, the therapist, while on a backpacking vacation, called the client to see how she was. Barb was deeply moved by the therapist's concern. It was a turning point in the therapy. The suicidal ideation stopped and Barb went off the medication and actively addressed several areas of her life in a positive way. Six months after termination, Barb wrote to the therapist and offered her unsolicited perceptions of the therapy and the therapist's concern:

When I thought about the therapy, and what I missed, I picture myself in your office, just telling you stuff and you listening. And I thought of you backpacking and stopping to call *me*! And I thought of the time you drove to your office to get my phone number when I didn't leave it on your home machine. And every time I called you, you called me back. It didn't always help, but *you were there*. And I realized that is just what a little girl would want from her daddy, what I had been missing all my life and wanting so badly. Finally, when I was 39 years old, someone gave it to me . . . But I sure am glad I got to know what it feels like to have someone care about me in that way. It was a beautiful gift you gave me. It's ironic that you also made me realize how much God loves me. When you called me that weekend you went backpacking, I thought to myself, "If a human can do that for me, then I believe what the Bible says about us all the time." . . . So, thanks for loving me—because that's what you did.

Although the special significance of the phone calls was unknown until the letter was received, it was apparent that relationship factors were of paramount importance. The client used the therapist's call as an opportunity for change. Many other aspects of this case could be highlighted, but it was the client's interpretation of the relationship that seemed primary. Our experience, as well as the empirical literature, support this conclusion. Clients who give high ratings to the alliance are very likely to be successful in achieving their goals.

The significance of client and common factors (over technique), the superiority of clients' perceptions in predicting outcomes (over therapists'), and the equivalence of outcome among therapy approaches offer a persuasive argument for more attention to the client's experience of the psychotherapeutic process. Understanding the client's subjective experience and phenomenological representation of the presenting problem, and placing that experience above any theoretical predilection, offers yet another way to accommodate therapy to the client's frame of reference.

ACCOMMODATING THE CLIENT'S THEORY OF CHANGE

The final dimension of the client's frame of reference encompasses the client's thoughts, beliefs, attitudes, and feelings about the impetus for therapy (the problem or situation), its causes, and how therapy may best address the client's goals for treatment. This is the client's theory of change.

This perspective builds on the MRI concept of position, or the client's beliefs, values, and attitudes that specifically influence the presenting problem and the client's participation in therapy (Fisch, Weakland, & Segal, 1982). The approach of the MRI, and specifically John Weakland, provides a practical application of taking the client's view seriously (Hoyt, 1994).

The client's theory of change contains most, if not all, of the trappings of any psychological theory, that is, etiology, treatment, and prognosis. Accommodating the client's theory requires the therapist to first learn it and then adopt it as the map for how therapy will progress. Accommodation means that all therapist activities and interventions are made congruous with or suitable to that theory, unless an agreement with the client is attained regarding any intervention outside of the client's theory.

Contrast the client's theory with the therapist's treatment orientation. Theory-driven approaches consist of either general notions regarding the cause of problems (e.g., symptoms are surface manifestations of intrapsychic conflict, symptoms are homeostatic mechanisms regulating a dysfunctional subsystem) or predetermined and specific explanatory schemes (e.g., fixated psychosexual development, triangulation), which are addressed across cases to solve problems (Held, 1986, 1991). Cause and effect are either specified or implied by way of theoretical constructs of formal theory. Those constructs provide the content, which become the invariant explanations of the problems that bring clients to therapy.

In theory-driven approaches to psychotherapy, the theoretical orientation of the therapist is hierarchically superior to the frame of reference of the client. This formal theory structures problem definition as well as outcome criteria. The more theory-driven the approach, the more theory-directed the goals become.

The client presents with a complaint, and the therapist will overtly or covertly recast the complaint within the language of the therapist's theory. The therapist's reformulation of the complaint into a specific preconceived content enables treatment to proceed down a particular path flowing from the formal theory.

Conversely, accommodating the client's frame of reference requires that the focus of the therapeutic conversation emerge from the theory of the client (Barbara Held calls this the client's informal theory). Recall the Bachelor (1991) study, which indicated the importance of not only the therapist-provided variables, but also the therapist's efforts to explore material that the client perceived as relevant. Clients want therapists to explore their theories.

Rather than reformulating the client's theory into the language of the therapist's orientation, we suggest the exact opposite: that therapists elevate the client's perceptions and experiences above theoretical conceptualizations, thereby allowing the client to direct therapeutic choices. Such a process all but guarantees the security of a strong alliance.

THE CLIENT'S THEORY AND THE THERAPEUTIC ALLIANCE

Accommodating the client's theory appears warranted given the importance of client perceptions to outcome (Bachelor, 1991; Gurman, 1977; Horowitz et al., 1984) and the large body of evidence demonstrating that the alliance, as rated by client, therapist, and third-party perspectives, is the best predictor of psychotherapy outcome (Alexander & Luborsky, 1986; Marmar et al., 1986).

Gaston (1990) summarizes the alliance into four components: (1) the client's affective relationship with the therapist, (2) the client's capacity to purposely work in therapy, (3) the therapist's empathic understanding and involvement, and (4) client-therapist agreement in the goals and tasks of therapy. While the first and third components reiterate the importance of the relationship and the therapist-provided variables, the client's participation and agreement on goals and tasks refers to the congruence between the client's and the therapist's beliefs about *how people change in therapy* (Gaston, 1990).

Accommodating the client's theory develops a strong alliance by promoting therapist agreement with client beliefs about change as well as the goals and tasks of therapy. The therapist attends to what the client considers important, addresses what the client indicates as significant, and accommodates both in- and out-of-session intervention to accomplish goals specified by the client.

The Case of Molly

Returning to Molly one final time, she explains how not securing her input missed the mark. It is clear that Molly's and the therapist's beliefs about how people change in therapy were not congruent.

T: I knew you'd seen other therapists about not being able to sleep in your room, but yet . . .

M: It didn't help. I didn't want to do it. They weren't my ideas and they didn't seem right. Well, like my other therapist said, "Let's try this for 5 minutes, then go for 10 minutes, then 15, then go for the whole night." I did it once and I decided, "This isn't helping!" I did it for 5 minutes and neglected to do it for 10, and then I didn't do it for 15, and then I didn't do it for half an hour. I didn't want to do that thing, so I basically ignored it.

In Molly's therapy, a deliberate effort was made to forge an alliance. Molly had become a veteran of failed therapy, misery, and the struggle for change at the ripe age of 10. In conversation, she made it clear that her goal was to get out of mother's room and sleep without nightmares. The therapist accepted her goal. Similarly, her proposed solution for her problem was welcomed. Since the previous interventions were not her own and were unilaterally formed, as the alliance literature would predict, they fell flat. Her own intervention worked and her pride was restored.

CONCLUSION

Setting aside the intellectual appeal of the rich and diverse models of psychotherapy, the seductiveness of flashy technique promising magical cures, and the charismatic "masters," research suggests that successful outcome occurs by creating a space for clients to use their resources, ensuring clients' positive experience of the alliance, and accommodating therapy to clients' views of what is relevant. *Each client, therefore, presents the therapist with a new theory to learn and a different therapeutic course to pursue.*

Influenced by four decades of investigation of successful outcome and recent findings regarding the alliance, we propose an intentional accommodation of the therapeutic process to the client's frame of reference and a deliberate promotion of a client-directed psychotherapy. Empowering existing client strengths and building a strong alliance are not passive therapist postures, but rather require a focused effort to conduct psychotherapy within the context of the client's frame of reference. Outcome research suggests that therapy devote itself more to the individual client's construction of what constitutes success (Duncan & Moynihan, 1994). This book applies this empirical suggestion to impossible cases.

CLINICAL METHODS

may my heart always be open to little
birds who are the secrets of living
whatever they sing is better than to know
and if men should not hear them men are old

may my mind stroll about hungry
and fearless and thirsty and supple
and even if it's sunday may i be wrong
for whenever men are right they are not young

and may myself do nothing usefully
and love yourself so more than truly
there's never been quite such a fool who could fail
pulling all the sky over him with one smile

E. E. Cummings

CHAPTER 3

Working with Impossibility:
Therapist Considerations

Daring as it is to investigate the unknown, even more so it is to question the known.

Kaspar

VETERANS OF UNSUCCESSFUL THERAPY are casualties of the mental health system. They have often been disbelieved and their distress discredited—not because their helpers are intentionally insensitive, but rather because of the obstacles that the process of helping itself often provide. When treatment is ineffective, it typically furthers the client's burden by proving the problem's characterological origin. Impossibility can sometimes be retaliatory explanations for failed interactions with clients.

The first step in creating an efficient therapeutic encounter with psychotherapy veterans is to assume that, in some way, therapy has failed to understand and address their desires. Therapy progresses by allowing the prevailing conventions about psychopathology and theoretical correctness to fade into the background, while empowering the client's frame of reference to expand into the foreground.

This chapter presents general principles for approaching impossible cases that address the pathways introduced in Chapter 1. These principles include: taking your own pulse, avoiding attribution creep, cultivating a beginner's mind, and preserving dignity at (almost) any cost.

37

TAKING YOUR OWN PULSE

How much pain have cost us the evils which have never happened.
Thomas Jefferson

Words are granted the power to induce intense emotional reactions. Merely mentioning a person's name, for instance, may trigger an experience of love or hate, respect or revulsion, joy or sorrow. One can readily contrast what comes to mind with these few well-known examples: George Washington, Benedict Arnold, Winston Churchill, Adolph Hitler.

In the mental health professions there are other names we know and use. They are not proper names, but designations given to the conditions, symptoms, and complaints clinicians set out to address. Many of these names also have the power to induce strong emotion. Schizophrenia and the common and overused term, borderline, are good illustrations. For practitioners, these names frequently arouse apprehension, tension, and wariness. They also may kindle, as described in the first chapter, the anticipation of impossibility.

It is unrealistic to expect that therapists could or should make themselves insensitive or invulnerable to the words and the experiences that help shape emotion. Even so, there are steps that practitioners may take to offset the more provocative aspects not only of diagnostic labeling, but also of clients' sometimes troubling presentations, stories, or histories. Collectively, these steps are called *taking your own pulse*.

The goal of taking your own pulse is to position or prepare oneself to withstand the recruitment of anxiety, urgency, pessimism, and over-responsibility. These states, moods, or expectations contribute to the prediction or anticipation of impossibility — an unwanted and corrosive perception when working with the therapy veteran.

Though taking your own pulse is meant as a metaphor, it is also a concrete suggestion for something to do. Therapists may actually want to take their pulse when one of the four horsemen of impossibility (i.e., anxiety, urgency, pessimism, and over-responsibility) appears. The idea is to introduce a pause, a moment of composure and reflection, whenever emotion or the motivation to act hastily threatens to get the best. Keeping in mind that impossibility may, in part, be sponsored by our own attitudes and interventions gives reason to preserve self-possession. Spending as much time as possible out of the depths of our limbic systems helps us, helps our clients, and defeats the presumption of impossibility.

In applying the principle of taking your own pulse, there are no prescribed methods or techniques to follow. Each therapist is free to develop a repertoire for clearing emotional cobwebs. In developing them, one is limited only by creativity and respect for the client's experience.

The steps for taking your own pulse may be divided into three broad categories: actions to take on your own, with others, and with the client.

Actions to Take on Your Own

Joel Bergman, a colorful and respected clinician practicing in New York, is also an accomplished piano player. In his workshops he says that in situations when he finds a therapy tough going, he may move from his seat before the client to the piano he keeps in his office. There, he begins to play until his clarity and perspicacity return.

Though Bergman has cultivated a flair for drama and the unexpected in his work, a reputation probably not lost on those who see him professionally, he knows when to act on his own to keep his therapeutic wits. Some therapists have referred to this as becoming "centered." Sheldon Kopp (1977), the well-known humanistic therapist in Washington, DC, described the process with the title of his book, *Back to One*.

Perhaps a more practical method already familiar to all therapists is to practice a variation of deep muscle relaxation. Of course, the full progressive relaxation protocol need not be followed; simply crossing one's legs at the ankles, tensing, releasing the tension, then feeling the difference is often enough. Breathing and exhaling at a measured cadence may also prove useful. The important point is to encourage relaxation, breaking any "trance" arising from the anxious or pessimistic anticipation of impossibility.

In recent years, therapists of the structural, strategic, and solution-focused traditions have used a brief recess from the therapy session to gain distance and perspective, and to think through any intervention or suggestion before proposing it to the client. Recognizing that the heat of the moment or impulse to do or say something helpful may make matters worse, these therapists will temporarily excuse themselves to review their findings, develop a strategy, and gain a "breather." Clients are usually told at the beginning of the therapy of the clinician's plan to break; in our experience, rarely do clients object to this practice. The time can also be used by asking the client to think over carefully what happened in the session and to consider what will be the next step for improvement. Not surprisingly, when the therapist returns from the break, an expectancy often arises between clinician and client that whatever is now said may hold greater importance for the work.

If taking a break proves unfeasible, and if emotion or the pressure to act is mounting, time for oneself may be gained by saying to the client, "Please give me a moment to consider carefully what you are saying." Then, take a few minutes to become collected. If the pause feels uncomfortable, jotting down observations, questions to be asked, or intervention suggestions may dispel any interpersonal awkwardness. Clients, no matter what their presenting complaint and presumed level of ego organization, almost always respond well to good manners and appreciate the therapist's efforts to understand them. Hasty interventions prompted by anxiety and urgency are frequently not worth the effort.

Another approach for acting on one's own is to keep attention riveted on the process of the session. Here, we remember the words of the philosopher Wittgenstein, "Don't think: Look!" Anxiety or other perturbing experiences may be used as signals or cues to concentrate on what is taking place in the meeting with the client. As the Wittgenstein quote implies, thinking—especially in this context, frightening or other trying thoughts about the client—interferes with looking, with observation and listening.

Rather than using one's senses to become bowled over by emotion, a greater dividend is earned by looking for what works. For example, does sitting closer to the client or farther away make a helpful difference? Is the client favorably responsive to certain words or phrases? Does using the client's first name invite closeness or is it experienced as a discourtesy (Everstine & Everstine, 1983)? Are reflections of affect more effective at unfolding the client's story than reflections of the therapist's cognitive understanding?

We might liken the therapy of impossible cases to crossing a rope bridge in a rain forest. It may feel that irreversible failure is only a quick slip away. Yet, what usually supports success is taking time, watching where one is going, measuring headway one hand after another, and keeping one's eyes on the goal. Thinking about how easily it will be to plunge beneath the canopy or the difficulty of the task ahead lessens the chances of making it to the other side. In short, noticing what promotes progress offers a surer bet for a successful conclusion.

One last recommendation for acting on one's own is to offer no intervention. If stumped, befuddled, or clueless regarding what a client might do about a complaint, it is better to say, "I don't know," than to intervene. Again, offering quickly conceived explanations, giving task assignments, or acting with a false assurance born in anxiety, may risk getting on the conga line of failure with the veteran.

Going slowly and suggesting circumspection in the face of what feels like overwhelming circumstances may at first seem grossly out of step with the wish to relieve pain. Yet, calm can be contagious. Saying, "We can value this time together," "We can set a sensible pace for change," "We can now consider as much as there is to know about you, before acting," may provide the much needed eye in a long-standing storm.

Actions to Take With Others

What feels like torment alone, in the company of others becomes a shared experience — a bulwark against anxiety. In this respect, we have found that taking your own pulse can be easier done when in the company of like-minded therapists.

A valuable approach for defeating worry and precipitous action is to conduct therapy with a team. Recent years have seen a revolution in the use of the two-way mirror in clinical practice. Having trusted colleagues behind the mirror or observing through a remote monitor can remove immediate pressures arising from the mood of a session. One is free to conduct the therapy, knowing that anytime the team can phone or walk-in with guidance on pace and direction.

An added bonus of the team is having access to them during a break. As much as taking a break on one's own can be helpful, a break with the team present allows the therapist a convenient forum for discussing the session, reviewing what worked, and gaining additional ideas on suggestions for the client. For their part, clients often respond positively to the idea that a team of therapists is consulting and working for them. Sometimes, we hear, "That's good. My problem requires many doctors" or "More heads are better than one." Offering the client the choice to meet the team or hear (or participate in) the team's discussion is recommended to assuage any fears that clients may have about the treatment team process.

Though teamwork is not an efficient measure to use always, it may prove very cost-effective in situations where previous therapies have not taken or the client is facing a more expensive, restrictive, and time-extensive alternative.

Should an on-site treatment team be unavailable, therapists can still consult with a colleague before proceeding, saying to the client, "I want to take what you've told me today, think about it, and carefully discuss it with some of my colleagues before we proceed. When we next get together, I'll share what they had to say in detail."

Besides acting as a step-down transformer for the therapist's anxiety, a treatment team or consultant may serve as an "alter-ego" or auxiliary voice for the primary treater. As it is often said that you cannot be a prophet in your own land, some clients may perceive a message from the consultant/s as having more credibility than if the identical message or explanation came from the therapist. Perhaps most importantly, using consultation shows caring; that is, the therapist knows how to ask, receive, and relate recommendations for the veteran's behalf. It is like saying to the client, "I care enough about your situation that I'll find whatever help *I* need to see that you get the help *you* need."

Using consultants also shows a lack of arrogance. Perhaps nothing is more detrimental for therapy than a practitioner who proposes, then sticks to an explanation or treatment strategy that falls flat with the veteran. Admitting that one needs another opinion or additional ideas models problem-solving and flexibility.

Actions to Take With the Client

As mentioned before, we have heard from our "impossible" clients that their opinions and ideas about their condition or presenting complaint have been rejected, ignored, or filtered through a patronizing attitude. Therefore, the simple act of saying to them, "I am confused (puzzled, worried, feeling anxious, etc.) about what you are describing. Will you help me to understand this further?" may be the first time that they have been invited to be co-participants or partners in their therapy.

Some time ago, one of us was leading a team of interns at a university training center. The client was no stranger to suicide. Hospitalized several times for suicidal ideation and attempts, her continued talk about self-destruction bound up the team. Concern about her potential lethality preoccupied our deliberations—so much so the team was beginning to feel as hopeless and depressed as the client. The logjam broke when the primary therapist shared with the client his and the team's apprehension about her situation and worry over saying or doing, or neglecting to say or do, something that would push her over the edge. Once she heard the team's admission, she said that she, too, was troubled by the role of suicide in her life. In later sessions, she began to take steps out of depression that were life-enhancing and life-preserving. What made the difference here is when the team treated the client as an equal, not as a fragile, porcelain doll whose continued existence depended on their every move.

AVOIDING ATTRIBUTION CREEP

> Observe things as they are and don't pay attention to other people.
> Huang Po

In the first chapter, theory countertransference was introduced as a reliable and robust pathway to impossibility. Theories, especially those invoking ideas of pathology, disorder, and dysfunction, have acted as powerful lenses for focusing therapists' attention. Curiously, though the disciplines of psychiatry, psychology, social work, and counseling all claim to promote health and competency, they have largely made a cult out of their clients' *in*competence (Miller et al., 1997). This is not meant to derogate the mental health professions; it is simply a statement of fact. Theories of therapy are principally theories of psychopathology (see Held, 1991).

In concert with diagnostic labeling, theory countertransference encourages *attribution creep*. This means that no matter how committed a therapist is to seeing a client objectively, the client will eventually take on the characteristics and qualities defined by the therapist's theory. For example, if a clinician subscribes to the work of Kohut, the client will be seen as narcissistically wounded, in need of a "holding environment" and "transmuting internalizations." Treatment perforce will be protracted as the client will require slow mending under the sustained empathic ministrations provided by the psychotherapist. Similarly, if a clinician is convinced that psychological symptoms are the result of chemical imbalances—excesses and shortages of certain neurotransmitters—then medication is the answer. In this case, the client suffers from an illness and, perhaps other than complying with the drug regimen, has no active part to play in promoting recovery. The client becomes a hapless victim of a biology gone awry.

As with diagnostic categorization, theories can inhibit work of therapy. Theories are not "stand-ins" for reality. They are "shorthands." Indeed, they are abstractions used for making sense of the sometimes bewildering array of information gathered in conducting therapy. Theories also provide road maps, directions to take for finding a way to a successful outcome.

Because theories are abstractions, their usefulness is not guaranteed. When the therapy goes well, there is a natural tendency to say that the theory is affirmed. Nonetheless, when the therapy falters, often the theory is upheld at the expense of the client. This then becomes fertile ground for attribution creep.

Using the example of a classical psychoanalysis, if the therapy totters, there would be a temptation to see the client as more damaged than originally thought. It is not that the method does not fit; the analysand's personality may be too primitive to weather the frustration inherent in the psychoanalytic situation—a setting constructed in part on the interpretation of transference, the emotional detachment of the psychoanalyst, and an enthusiastic adherence to theoretical dogma. Not surprisingly, in years past, if a psychoanalysis was failing, the "patient" would begin to be seen as "latent schizophrenic."

To avoid the influence of attribution creep, a pragmatic rule may be applied to theory. If the theory promotes improvement, helps clients achieve their therapeutic goals, and provides room to be questioned by both the therapist and client, then use it. On the other hand, if the theory claims more truth than warranted, stereotypes clients who fail to profit by its application, and plainly is not working, then jettison it. With close to 400 contenders in the therapeutic theory market, there is likely to be one out there more amicable to the veteran.

Another reminder for defeating attribution creep is that despite how dire the prospects may appear for the client, change is inevitable. Tracking the natural history of certain "incurable disorders," we now know that improvement takes place. For instance, long-term follow-up studies of people diagnosed as chronic schizophrenics show that 50–60% return to normal or are significantly improved as they grow older (Harding, Zubin, & Strauss, 1987). Apparently, the assumed biology of schizophrenia does not determine destiny.

Still another way to defend the therapy against theory counter-transference is to take care in reading others' clinical notes and records. It is common with a case considered impossible to accumulate a bloated folder — filled with notes, test reports, and summaries — all giving rich testimony to the impossibility of the client's condition. While it is responsible and prudent to request prior records, there is no rule that says that therapists have to read immediately anybody else's opinions about the client before forming their own impressions.

When a therapy fails, the clinical record will contain many plausible sounding explanations for the failure, often exonerating the therapists and their preferred theories. In these instances, nothing is to be gained by priming an already powerful pump for attribution creep. It is better to approach a case fresh, open to the opportunities that present themselves now.

CULTIVATING A BEGINNER'S MIND

In the beginner's mind there are many possibilities, but in the expert's there are few.

Shunryu Suzuki

Experience tells us that should we encounter a large, fast-moving gray-hued animal, with thick pounding legs, big floppy ears, a long trunk, tusks, emitting a loud trumpeting sound, we'd best move aside and let it pass. It is probably an elephant. Here experience has high predictive value.

However, what if the next day as therapists, our clinical experience tells us that when we encounter this kind of client, with this

complaint, we apply this technique or model? The results may not
be as certain or successful. Unfortunately, it is frequently true that
despite the best of intentions, experience will lead therapists to hold
onto a technique or method though the result is a floundering therapy. Experience then is a two-edged sword. What one gains in practice and conviction may be at the price of flexibility and openness.

With the proliferation of therapy approaches and schemes, the
mental health professions have found that one size does not fit all.
Yet, once in a therapy session, it is easy to become convinced that
with more time, patience, and more aggressive application of a given
clinical strategy, the client's problem will yield. After all, we say to
ourselves, "I've seen this work before." In Chapter 1, illustrated with
the case of Molly, *doing more of the same was identified as a pathway to impossibility.*

At times, doing more of the same may be hard to avoid. Once one
commits to a course of action, other factors, besides experience, may
come into play that keep an ineffective solution in motion. As an
example, pride may force the hand of a therapist. For some, to avoid
admitting that one is wrong or has made a mistake can sponsor a
deeper devotion to a therapy strategy. This is especially true if the
case is high profile or is drawing the attention of other professionals
(Chapter 9 provides an example).

Theory countertransference has a part too. TC has its latest incar-
nation in what is being called "solution-forced" therapy (Nylund &
Corsiglia, 1994). Therapists, entranced with the alleged therapeutic
power of the solution-focused model, may pummel a client with
searches for exceptions, miracle and scaling questions, and related
tactics until the client leaves (see Chapter 7).

To answer the challenge of doing more of the same, a "beginner's
mind" is recommended. Cultivating a beginner's mind means that no
matter how many cases of "complaint x" one has seen, *this case is
new.* Contrary to therapist desires for and marketing hype about
"treatments of choice," prescriptive approaches for specific problems
are based more in myth than empirical verification (Miller et al.,
1997).

It also means that no matter how many unsuccessful therapies the
veteran has undergone, this one may be different. A beginner's mind
suggests that as therapists we do not allow our clinical experience to
fossilize our openness to possibility.

A quick rule of thumb for keeping a beginner's mind nimble is, if by the third session with the client there is no progress, then it is time to do something different. That is, it is time to begin anew. The rule helps to keep the therapist attending to what is happening and working in the session, in the present with this client versus in memories of bygone sessions with others whose situation may closely resemble, but have nothing to do with, the current client's dilemma.

When we find ourselves feeling stuck with a client, we like to remind ourselves of the words of *Star Trek*'s Mr. Spock, "There are always possibilities."

PRESERVING DIGNITY AT (ALMOST) ANY COST

I'd rather fight than switch.
Advertising Tagline for Tareyton Cigarettes

In cultures different from our own, there are traditions requiring a strong deference to authority. In American society, the relationship to authority is more muddled. On one hand, there is a yearning for strong and capable leadership (witnessed in the veneration of Abraham Lincoln and Harry Truman) and simultaneously a wish to criticize, oppose, and even topple those that would exert influence or control. Looking back, this country was, in part, founded to pursue self-determination, freedom, and dignity. We fondly remember and embrace revolutionary slogans such as, "Give me liberty or give me death" and "Don't tread on me." The legacy is that for Americans, being ordered about or "dictated to" is equal to oppression.

Therapy is not immune from the pressures of general culture. Many clients, whatever the severity of their situations, continue to maintain membership in the cultural mainstream and listen to cultural values and themes. So, it is not surprising that despite the duration and intensity of their pain, they will not collaborate in a therapy that, in their perception, pushes them around, assails their personal honor, or intimates that they are any less for the predicament that brings them to our offices.

It is hard for therapists to avoid "oneupmanship" with clients. Our education and professional societies reinforce the idea of our expertness and authority. Advanced degrees, expensive training, supervision, licensing tests—all the myriad trials of passage for becoming a therapist confer a special status. Our commitment to helping and relieving distress also prompts us to act, to change our clients or their circumstances. Sometimes, it is as though we develop big helper hands comprised of all thumbs. And, in our dedicated efforts to remove the pain, clients may feel they are *getting* the treatment.

By the time veterans become veterans, it is easy to see how they will be in a mood to defend their dignity. There is an excellent chance they have been subjected to multiple mental status exams and asked about the most private and intimate aspects of their lives. In addition, they have completed intake forms, interpreted inkblots, made up stories from picture cards, filled out "objective" personality tests of hundreds of items, been placed on wait-lists, seen residents, interns, and trainees (only to have those people leave after they formed relationships with them), and waited more. Many have also been placed on scores of medications with unpleasant side effects, hospitalized, discharged, and readmitted. That they continue to come for therapy at all bespeaks a core of strength or hope unblemished.

As our clients may come prepared to preserve their dignity at any cost, we would do well to adopt an attitude that allows them to save face and self-worth. This position is not construed as legerdemain, an interpersonal tactic for winning the battle of resistance (as discussed in the MRI brief strategic therapy of Fisch et al., 1982). Rather, it reflects a genuine effort to provide the conditions for a person who has been deindividuated (Wright, 1991) by earlier treatment experiences to reindividuate—to become a person once more.

It is probably impossible to remove the power differential in the therapy relationship stacked in favor of the therapist. Nevertheless, it is possible to approach the veteran as a human being first, and as a diagnostic category or "treatment resistant" case last.

While this may sound obvious, trite, or naive, in an era when the profession is inundated with new brands of therapy, a steady stream of DSMs, anxieties over reimbursement, practice autonomy, and the future of health care, it is easier than ever before to misplace the person of the veteran. Perhaps it is this last pathway to impossibility that is most important to resist. This is why we chose to think of the "multiple problem, high-risk, resistant, chronic, barracuda, character-disordered" client as a veteran. Calling our clients veterans helped us remove blinders that inhibited approaching them as human beings.

Creating the conditions for clients to retain or rebuild their dignity has already been discussed (see Duncan et al., 1992; Hubble & Solovey, 1994; Miller et al., 1997) and will be elaborated further in this volume. As a brief refresher and preview, the following guidelines are offered:

1. *The client is the hero in the "drama" of therapy.* There are no great therapists, only great clients and therapists working together.
2. *Therapy is not done* to *a client.* It is an interpersonal exchange (event) in which emphasis is placed foremost on the quality of the client's participation.
3. *Interventions are not the "deal" in therapy.* Interventions are extensions of the therapeutic alliance and cannot be separated from the relationship in which they occur.
4. *The therapist suggests, the client chooses.* The therapist offers explanations, theories, or intervention approaches as suggestions for the client to consider and then accept, modify, or discard.

A FINAL NOTE

The pathways to impossibility can defeat us and our clients. They are not so powerful, however, that we must always follow them. Resisting their siren call comes, in part, from being prepared; that is, having at one's disposal a plan and set of procedures to follow. This chapter presented some ideas about attitudes and actions that we have adopted to avoid the blind alleys of impossibility. We encourage you to develop your own methods.

And yet, the strongest weapon in overcoming impossibility is the belief that it can be done. This belief or expectation for success, as hopefully is illustrated in the chapters that follow, is manifested in our unswerving trust in clients and our unbridled faith in the therapeutic alliance.

CHAPTER 4

Conversations with Impossibility: Making the Impossible Possible

> It is easier to discover a deficiency in individuals, in states, and in Providence, than to see their real import and value.
>
> Hegel

WE PREFER CALLING WHAT WE DO with clients conversing, or conversation, rather than interviewing (de Shazer, 1988; Goolishian & Anderson, 1987). Interviewing implies something done to clients rather than with them, and connotes an expert gathering information for evaluative purposes (e.g., diagnostic or mental status interview). Consequently, interviewing provides an inaccurate description *if* therapy intends to be nonjudgmental, collaborative, and to encourage maximum client participation.

Conversation, on the other hand, is the oral *exchange* of sentiments, observations, opinions, or ideas (*Webster's Collegiate Dictionary*, 1993). Conversation enlists client participation in a process of exploring the client's frame of reference (hereafter called world), discovering possibilities for a better future, and validating the client.

Exploring the client's world gives rise to opportunities for the collaborative discovery of new directions. Conversing with clients not only creates possibilities for change, more importantly, it also defines therapy as a caring, empathic, and validating environment that is committed to clients' achieving personal goals.

Conversation removes the artificial boundary between relationship and technique. Butler and Strupp (1986) assert that, "The com-

plexity and subtlety of psychotherapeutic processes cannot be reduced to a set of disembodied techniques because techniques gain
their meaning and, in turn, their effectiveness from the particular
interaction of the individuals involved" (p. 33).

Conversation, therefore, is an interpersonal event that links technique to the client's perceptions of the relationship and the client's
theory of change. Technique without such a link is like eating the
meringue of a pie apart from the filling and crust—bland and unful-
filling, lacking form, substance, and value (Miller et al., 1997).

This chapter provides a pragmatic description of making the impossible possible through accommodating and honoring the client's
theory of change. Two cases bearing the diagnosis of borderline
personality disorder exemplify our points and provide clinical relevance.

EXPLORING THE CLIENT'S WORLD:
LEARNING THE CLIENT'S THEORY OF CHANGE

The client's world is central to all else that occurs in treatment.
Exploring the client's world does not require listening with a "third
ear." It does require the therapist to remove therapy models out of
his or her "ears" and pay close attention to the client, without recast-
ing everything into the sometimes narrow confines of psychological
or theoretical constructs.

Exploring the client's world has three objectives:

1. To enlist client participation
2. To ensure the client's positive experience of the relationship and
    therapy itself
3. To learn the client's theory of change

In support of the first two objectives, consider the conclusion of
Orlinsky et al. (1994) in their extensive review of the process-
outcome literature:

The quality of the patient's participation in therapy stands out as the most
important determinant of outcome. . . . The therapist's contribution toward helping the patient achieve a favorable outcome is made mainly
through empathic, affirmative, collaborative, and self-congruent engage-

ment with the patient. . . . These consistent process-outcome relations, based on literally hundreds of empirical findings, can be considered *facts* established by 40-plus years of research on psychotherapy. (p. 361)

While the client's participation and positive evaluation are critical to success for all cases (Miller et al., 1997), veterans of impossibility require extra encouragement and special attention because of their prior negative experiences in treatment. Client participation and positive evaluation are greatly enhanced and almost guaranteed by honoring the client's theory. Honoring the client's theory makes the difference with impossible cases.

The Client's Resources and Ideas

Exploring the client's resources and ideas is especially important with veterans of impossibility because they tend to be viewed as not having any. Just peruse, for example, the personality disorder section of *DSM-IV*, or read the case notes of a failed case. One will hardly find anything that is either kind or respectful. Indeed, there is likely no mention of what a client does well.

Consider Katherine, a 28-year-old homemaker who was diagnosed with borderline personality disorder. Katherine had been in therapy on and off since she was a teenager. She had been hospitalized many times for suicide attempts, mostly drug overdoses, and had been treated for drug dependence and anorexia. However, she believed that most of this turbulent history was behind her. Katherine re-entered therapy for depression and her perceptions that she was incompetent at relationships because she either was a doormat to others or was "inappropriate" and out of control from time to time.

She had just terminated a therapeutic relationship of 2 years when she was referred to us by a friend at church. The previous therapist was well-known as a character-disorder specialist. Katherine experienced many changes during the two years, including the birth of her daughter, becoming a Christian, many conflicts with her in-laws, and the break-up of her best friendship. In the first session, Katherine reported that she had terminated therapy for two reasons: She was not making progress and she was offended by the therapist's suggestion that Katherine delay her career goal to be a teacher because of her instability in relationships.

Exploring Katherine's world revealed a variety of successes, changes, and ideas about her concerns. She discussed the joys and demands of motherhood and her newfound Christianity. Katherine found competence and self-respect in both areas. Most notable was her report of standing up to her long-time friend, who seemed to take every opportunity to make Katherine the butt of jokes and ridicule. Although Katherine was saddened by the loss of the friendship, she felt very positive about the way she handled herself. She saw her actions as indicative of an emerging new view of herself.

Highlighting Katherine's resources and ideas provided a sharp contrast to her previous experience in therapy. Katherine seemed to enjoy the discussion and became animated and engaged. As we will see, Katherine's existing resources and past successes become central to a successful outcome.

In our work we embrace the strong probability that clients not only have all that is necessary to resolve problems, but also may have already solved them, started to solve them, or have a very good idea about how to do it (recall Molly). Questions that highlight previous successes and competencies and elicit the client's hunches and educated guesses encourage participation, emphasize the client's input, and provide direct access to the client's theory of change. Such questions also cast clients in their deserved role as the primary agents of change.

Listening for and being curious about clients' resources and ideas does not mean that the therapist ignores clients' pain or assumes a cheerleading attitude, but rather that the therapist listens to the whole story: the confusion and the clarity, the suffering and the endurance, the pain and the coping, the desperation and the desire.

Exploring the client's resources and ideas is accomplished by:

- viewing client as healthy, capable, and competent.
- recognizing your dependence on client resources and ideas for successful outcome.
- making client participation central to all therapeutic moves.

Respect for client abilities and ideas invites participation. Participation breeds success.

Therapeutic Relationship/Alliance

Exploring the client's experience of the relationship is always important, but particularly with impossible cases because this is another aspect of therapy that has been often ignored. Just as clients with certain diagnoses are rarely appreciated for their capabilities or insights, clients considered impossible are infrequently courted for a favorable impression of therapy.

This is unfortunate because the client's view of the relationship/alliance is the *best* predictor of success, regardless of diagnosis (see Chapter 2). Altering clients' negative views of therapy from their previous experiences provides a giant step toward positive outcome. The cases of Molly and Barb are illustrative. Sometimes, all that is required for change to occur, even with seemingly intractable cases, is that simple shift in opinion regarding the therapist and the therapy.

Katherine came to therapy somewhat defensive because of her previous encounter with therapy. She later shared how demoralized she felt about the prior therapist's suggestion that she reconsider her career goals. The therapy unfortunately became another verification of her own perceptions of incompetence.

An initial stroke of luck created an early good impression. Because of baby-sitting problems, Katherine came to the first appointment with her infant daughter. She sheepishly asked the therapist if it was a problem. The therapist replied no, that he had a child the same age, and that he found children a pleasant reminder of life outside of therapy.

Katherine's demeanor shifted from reticent to relaxed as she explained that the other therapist had canceled the appointment when she brought the baby. Because it was obvious that Katherine did not like using a baby-sitter, the therapist encouraged her to bring her daughter. Katherine appreciated the therapist's flexibility and responded with active participation.

We are not suggesting that encouraging clients to bring their children is the answer to establishing a strong alliance. Rather, we are suggesting that flexibility and meeting client's needs are critical to success with impossible cases. We are willing to go a long way from traditional practice to gain client approval and participation because we know that those factors circumvent impossibility.

Ensuring the client's positive evaluation of the relationship occurs by:

- being likable, friendly, and responsive.
- making sure the client feels understood and that you fit the client's view of what your role should be.
- being flexible and allowing yourself to be many things to many people.

You are multidimensional and can utilize your own complexity for your clients by fitting their perceptions and responding to their needs.

The Client's Theory of Change

The client's theory is like any other in psychology; it describes and explains the problem from etiology to treatment. The client's theory contains the formula for success with impossible cases.

Exploring the client's theory of change requires the therapist to adopt a view of him- or herself as an alien from another planet. The "alien" therapist seeks a pristine understanding of an encounter with the client's idiosyncratic interpretations and experiences, having no other data base from which to draw conclusions.

The therapist patiently listens, permitting the client complete freedom to tell the whole story without interruption. Clients not only provide their views regarding the problem, but also their orientations toward life, their goals and ambitions, and the pressures and events surrounding their complaints. In short, clients unfold their philosophies of life.

The therapist learns and converses in the client's language and allows as much room as possible for the client's words and interpretations to emerge. We do not discourage "problem talk" in favor of "solution speak." Conversing in the client's language is respectful, demonstrates understanding, and prevents the imposition of different connotations not intended by the client.

We recommend taking notes during sessions so that the exact words that clients choose to describe problems and their desires for treatment can be recorded. Taking notes, when done in an unobtrusive way, conveys therapist interest in, as well as the importance of, the client's input.

In service of learning the client's theory, the MRI's basic elements of a first session are well-suited: the nature of the complaint, how the problem is being handled, and the client's minimal goals (Fisch et al., 1982).

Nature of the Complaint: Describing the Problem

The client's view of the nature of the complaint lays the foundation for everything that follows. The client determines the significance of the topics to be discussed. The therapist follows the client's lead in rendering the description of the problem. A context is thereby created that allows for the greatest client participation into defining the problem and its personal meaning.

It is often helpful to begin with a concrete description, specifically addressing the MRI question, "Who is doing what that presents a problem, to whom, and how does such behavior constitute a problem?" (Fisch et al., 1982, p. 70). Requesting examples is often the best way to get specific descriptions of the client's complaint (Fisch et al., 1982).

Although the "what" is important, "how" the problem constitutes a problem is more so. How a situation is a problem may seem plain — but is it really? Consider borderline personality disorder. What does it mean to the client? What is the client's experience of the problem? How is it a problem? Is it a relationship problem, a performance problem, a feeling problem, etc.? It is better for the therapist to inquire about the "how," rather than believing he or she really knows.

How the situation constitutes a problem leads to the client's personal experience and identifies what therapy should address; it provides a key element to the client's theory of change. The "how" keeps therapy relevant to the client's concerns and promotes therapist dependence on client participation.

Exploring Katherine's complaint revealed that she considered herself incompetent at relationships. She cited numerous examples of her tendency to be taken advantage of, as well as her blow-ups (and prior self-destructiveness) when she couldn't take anymore.

The "what" of Katherine's complaint had two components: (1) giving too much in relationships and being the butt of jokes, and (2) her inability to appropriately handle these situations of inequity and ridicule. When asked "how" her difficulties with relationships were a problem for her, Katherine replied that she was tired of being the "resident scapegoat" by her in-laws and wanted to be taken seriously.

Notice the words that Katherine used. "Resident scapegoat" provided an important indication of her theory of change. Katherine's reply to the "how" question reflected resentment and a strong position of being wronged by others. Perhaps more importantly, she identified the specific relationships that therapy should address. Exploring the nature of the complaint revealed not only the who, what, and how of Katherine's complaint, but also her motivations and expectations for therapy. Katherine's participation could be guaranteed by addressing how she could effectively manage and silence her in-laws when they attempted to ridicule her.

Exploring Exceptions and Solutions: Being Change-Focused

Exploring the nature of the complaint also entails pursuing when the problem isn't occurring (Berg & Miller, 1992; de Shazer, 1994; Miller et al., 1997). Exploring for exceptions to the problem, pretreatment change, and between-session improvements enables treatment to be "change-focused." Being change-focused means making a concerted effort to listen for and validate client change whenever and for whatever reason it occurs before or during treatment (Miller et al., 1996).

Exploring exceptions goes hand-in-hand with exploring solutions the client has tried previously (Watzlawick et al., 1974). Discussing previous solutions permits the therapist to avoid what has previously failed, amplify what has already worked, encourage the client's ideas to come forth, and further allows the client's perceptions to remain central.

Discussion of prior solutions also provides an excellent way for learning the client's theory of change. Exploring solutions enables the therapist to hear the client's evaluation of previous attempts and their fit with what the client believes to be helpful. Inquiring about prior solutions, therefore, allows the therapist to hear the client's frank appraisal of how change can occur.

Exploration of Katherine's exceptions and prior solutions proved to be very helpful, both in terms of learning her theory of change and providing a possibility for change. When asked about times in which she did not feel like the resident scapegoat and/or was taken seriously by her in-laws, she replied that it had never occurred. When questioned about exceptions in other conflicted relationships, Katherine reported a recent interaction with her former best friend. Although the encounter ended the relationship, Katherine felt pleased that she handled the conflict well and did not "buckle under" by apologizing or crying.

This very notable exception was a neon sign begging further elaboration. The next section will articulate how a course of action is discovered by expanding and building upon this exception.

Exploring previous solutions also revealed many blind alleys to avoid, as well as more information regarding Katherine's theory of change. Katherine tried just about every technique imaginable for directly communicating her distress to others about their criticisms and laughs at her expense. She read self-help books and attended seminars on effective communication. These approaches were not only ineffective, but were sometimes used as objects of ridicule. She had also participated in a co-dependency group for several months, but did not see its relevance to her life.

Unfolding these failed solutions not only permitted the therapist to avoid their recurrence, but also enabled the question of why Katherine believed that her straightforward and honest attempts had fallen flat. "Why" questions are direct conduits to the client's theory of change.

Katherine responded that her attempts did not work because her in-laws disapproved of her troubled past, and could only treat her like a "mental invalid." They did not want to change her role in the family as the "strange bird" that their son/brother married. During that discussion, Katherine made it clear that she really wanted to turn the tables on her relatives. Her motivations were very clear. Accommodating therapy to such strong client motivations makes therapy efficient.

Katherine also tried therapy. Although she identified similar problems and issues in the previous therapy, the therapist focused instead on Katherine's boundary confusion and poor sense of self. Katherine worked hard in therapy, but disagreed with the implication that she was totally at fault for her troubled relationships.

Katherine believed that she had changed over the years, especially since becoming a mother and a Christian, but that others were accustomed to her role as "mental" and everyone's fallguy. This was the second time Katherine said the word "role" and how others were locked into a limited way of thinking about her because of her treatment history. Katherine's theory was emerging with each question.

Katherine believed that she needed to change other's views of her role. In addition, she thought others to be partially to blame, that she was already in the process of changing, and that maybe she was not as incompetent as others thought.

Goals for Treatment: What the Client Wants

The final component of the exploring process is addressing the client's goals, hopes, and desires for therapy. *What the client wants from treatment may be the single most important piece of information that can be obtained.* It provides a snapshot of the client's theory and a route to a successful conclusion.

This information can be easily overlooked or taken for granted, especially with veterans of unsuccessful therapy. Previous treatment failure or an ominous diagnosis says nothing about an individual's goals for treatment. As our earlier discussion of motivation suggested, previous treatment failure is often caused by inattention to the client's desires and/or the theoretical imposition or assumption of goals. Successful outcome depends on the client's articulation of goals and therapy's commitment to those goals.

Exploring the client's view of success is characterized by careful listening combined with questions that define and redefine the client's goals for treatment. We depend on the client's participation to determine the goals for therapy. The more conscious, deliberate, and focused the attempt to draw the client into the goal formation and resolution process, the less significant explanatory models and theoretical correctness come to seem.

When we ask clients what they want out of therapy, what they want to be different, we give credibility to their beliefs and values regarding the problem and its solution. We are saying to them that their opinion is important and therapy is to serve them. As simple an act as it is, it invites clients to see themselves as a collaborator in making their lives better. It invites participation.

It is often helpful to encourage the client to think small (Fisch et al., 1982). A change in one aspect of an individual's life often leads to changes in other areas as well. The wonderful thing about thinking small is that the attainment of the small goal often becomes symbolic for resolving the entire problem; a metaphoric step into a new life.

Our favorite client story regarding small goals involves Bob, a

charming and witty salesperson who was depressed and not following through with sales calls. When questioned what would be different if he were not depressed, Bob replied that he would faithfully
make his sales appointments. When questioned about a step toward
that goal, Bob said that when he started flossing his teeth, he would
know he was on the right track. Bob began flossing his teeth and
making his appointments.

Bob's theory of depression included a step through good dental
hygiene. Because it was Bob's theory, not the therapist's, it worked.
Such is the nature of finding out what represents successful treatment
to the client. It is the unpredictability of client methods and accomplishments that makes this work fun.

Katherine's criterion for success was explored and re-explored.
Several different goals were discussed, but when asked to prioritize
her goals, Katherine identified being able to deal with her in-laws
better. The therapist asked Katherine to elaborate her criterion for
success, including what would be different if she were dealing with
her in-laws better. Katherine replied that she would not cry or blow
up, and she could handle the jokes and criticisms in stride.

DISCOVERING POSSIBILITIES: ACCOMMODATING THE CLIENT'S THEORY

Exploring the client's world promotes the discovery of possibilities
by both the client and the therapist. Every conversation sets the
occasion for unearthing new avenues out of the client's dilemma.

Because we are not out to influence particular meanings or distin-
guish between health, pathology, or any other explanatory concept,
there is a freedom to speculate and consider a variety of ideas. Some
ideas grow into relevant discussion, while others fade away as it
becomes apparent they are not helpful to pursue.

The kinds of questions asked and the answers obtained powerfully
determine the direction of therapy. They will promote change or
discourage it. Certainly, no one wants a blind alley, but still there
are many out there to be avoided.

The objective of the discovering process is to identify possibilities
(exceptions, solutions, connections, or conclusions) that (1) permit
a course of action to address the client's goals, or (2) through redefi-
nition, render the problem as no longer a problem.

Exceptions and Solutions

Pursuing exceptions to the complaint and the client's attempted solutions often results in the discovery of possibilities. Besides preventing the therapeutic pitfall of suggesting something that hasn't already worked, such a pursuit also offers the opportunity to discuss solutions that have worked previously, ones that are currently helping, or ones that the client may be considering (Heath & Atkinson, 1989).

Questions building upon exceptions, successful solutions, or the client's idea of an untried solution can result in different viewpoints or new directions to address the problem. Molly's response to the therapist's questioning her ideas about solution ultimately led to a successful outcome.

Once an exception or solution has been identified, the therapist asks other questions designed to unfold perspectives and expand resolve to address problematic situations. Such empowering questions enable the client to draw upon previous knowledge and often encourage him or her to experience a sense of self-efficacy.

Katherine identified a notable exception to her usual ways of handling criticism and her "fall guy" role. Katherine had received the customary put-downs by her best friend and had somehow laughed along with the jokes, although she was hurt by them. She also had refused, despite her friend's insistence and guilt induction, to go out of her way to pick up another friend to meet them for lunch. Katherine reported that her friend's dumbfounded response gave her the strength to pull it off.

The therapist asked how else she was able to pull it off, and Katherine gave a most fascinating answer: She said that it was like she was someone else, as if she were playing a different role. Energized by her friend's astonished reaction, Katherine played the part of someone confident and unaffected by criticism.

A long discussion ensued about the role she played, where it came from, and how she could implement that success with her in-laws. Both client and therapist actively contributed to the conversation, and a feeling of excitement, a sense of discovery, characterized the session. The therapist asked who Katherine thought she was playing, that is, was it someone in particular that she had in mind. Katherine indicated that it was no one specifically, just someone who was bright, witty, and "didn't take any crap" in a sophisticated way.

The therapist asked Katherine, if the role she played was a famous person, who would it be? The therapist explained that he once read an article (Coale, 1992) in which the client was asked to become a famous person, living or dead, that could handle the situation with which the client was having difficulty. The client had chosen Joan of Arc and it had been helpful. The therapist admitted that it sounded strange, but did anyone come to mind that would turn the tables on her in-laws and shatter her resident scapegoat role? The client responded with "Katherine Hepburn." When the client said her name, it was like treasure had been discovered. Both beamed with pleasure and anticipation.

The next session focused on writing the script for Katherine's role in an upcoming visit from the in-laws. Katherine decided to do all she could to look the part, including the Hepburn trademark scarf around her neck. The handling of the put-downs in a humorous and unaffected way was pursued, and the therapist suggested that Katherine take the jokes in stride by agreeing with, and exaggerating them.

For example, when asked the typical question of whether or not she was still seeing a shrink, Katherine might reply that yes she was, and in fact, her therapist increased her sessions because she was on the brink of a total psychotic break. Katherine nearly choked from laughter and most of the session was spent laughing and plotting. Katherine added that she could try the "agree and exaggerate" (Duncan & Rock, 1991) strategy with a slight Hepburn smile on her face.

Intervention versus Invention

The word "intervention" does not adequately describe the collaborative process that occurred between Katherine and the therapist. To intervene is to "come between by way of hindrance or modification" (*Webster's Collegiate Dictionary*, 1993). Just like "interviewing," it implies something done to clients rather than with them, and consequently overemphasizes the technical expertise of the therapist, inaccurately portraying what makes therapy successful. "Intervention" does not capture the dependence of technique on the client's resources and ideas or how technique is successful to the extent that it emerges from the client's positive evaluation of the relationship and accommodates the client's theory of change.

We favor the words "invent" and "invention." To invent is to "find or discover, to produce for the first time through imagination or ingenious thinking and experiment" (*Webster's Collegiate Dictionary*, 1993). Every technique is used for the first time, invented by clients to fit their circumstance. Clients are the inventors; we are their assistants.

The techniques used with Katherine (playing a role and agree and exaggerate) were inextricably related to her perceptions of the relationship and her theory of change. Katherine's description of her success with her friend stimulated the therapist's remembrance of the "pretend identity" technique (Coale, 1992). The technique was already a part of Katherine's reported success and she invented Hepburn as a further application. Similarly, she took the agree and exaggerate strategy and applied it as she perceived that Hepburn would apply it, with an accompanying disarming smile. The technique, as it is generally utilized, is accompanied by resignation, depression, or similarly nonsarcastic response (e.g., Duncan & Rock, 1991; Fisch et al., 1982). Both techniques were consequently applied in unique and ingenious ways, devised by the client to fit her idiosyncratic strengths and ideas. They were inventions, a result of Katherine's imagination and experimentation.

Connections and Conclusions

The understanding of any situation is an interpretive process and therefore open to input and revision. Conversing with clients unfolds and expands meaning and experience and actually cocreates new connections or conclusions for those experiences.

A major support for the significance of the conversational process comes from the experimental literature regarding memory. Memory can no longer be thought of as an archival system of specific memories or complete records of discrete episodes. Instead, memory is a process involving bits and pieces of information that are continually interpreted and reconstructed during the course of remembering. Memories and their meanings are not static, but are constantly evolving recreations (Rosenfield, 1988).

Clients relating their experiences to therapists, therefore, are reconstructing those experiences each time, enabling the possibility for alternative ways of understanding. Each articulation of the client's concerns presents an opportunity for a different experience of those concerns. A new connection or conclusion may be discovered that permits a course of action or renders the problem as no longer a problem.

Connections

Veterans of impossibility are sometimes overwhelming in their presentations of problems. These problems seem, at times, to fill the session so full that the therapist feels smothered, gasping for air. The much needed oxygen and breath of fresh air for both client and therapist come when the problem is connected to a description that states or implies that the presenting complaint is changeable.

Connections occur by way of linking, through questions and discussion, the client's stated concern to a therapy-resolvable definition of that concern. Recall that Katherine initially presented a problem of incompetence at relationships. Exploring her world and defining Katherine's view of success resulted in a description of the problem that permitted a course of action. The definition of the problem evolved from something abstract and difficult to change to handling her in-laws' criticisms in stride without crying or apologizing.

Connecting client presentations to relationship issues makes obvious sense in many cases because relationships are a frequent topic that clients bring to therapy. A joint focus by the client and the therapist on core personal relationships also makes empirical sense. In the Orlinsky et al. (1994) review, the authors suggest that positive outcome is enhanced when clients focus on life problems and core personal relationships. Perhaps the data are saying that therapy should pursue the real life concerns of clients, not the assumptions of theory.

Conclusions

Since meaning and experience are constantly open to revision, clients may reach conclusions that permit problem resolution or render the problem no longer a problem. Consider the case of Cindy. Because of traumatic circumstances, Cindy had been in therapy most of her life. At the age of 29, she had experienced 8 therapists. Cindy was a sexual abuse survivor and represented a remarkable example of strength and resilience. Cindy re-entered therapy because she didn't trust men. She believed her trust problem to be a character flaw and the final abuse issue to resolve.

Exploration of Cindy's trust problem permitted an ongoing possibility for different conclusions to be reached. Cindy shared a summary of her abusive history, which began at age 6 with her father, and occurred with uncles, cousins, and neighbors throughout her childhood. As an adult, Cindy had been raped and battered by her ex-husband, and sexually harassed by a therapist. Almost every man in her life, especially those who "loved" her and/or should be trustworthy, abused her.

Each time Cindy recounted one of her many abusive experiences, her view of her trust problem as a personal deficit to overcome seemed to lose credibility and other explanations seem to become more plausible. One of those explanations was that she had good reason to be openly skeptical. Her experience clearly demonstrated that many men are not worthy of her trust, especially those men who want to be close to her.

Cindy began expressing misgivings about the trust problem. The more the conversation unfolded, the more benefits to the trust problem became apparent. Not trusting men helped her not commit too fast and take care of herself better. Cindy concluded that the trust *issue* (not problem) was something to continually evaluate to make sure she wasn't closing herself off to relationships, but that it was okay for her to be reluctant to invest her trust. The meaning of the client's experience unfolded and expanded until ultimately she concluded that she did not have a problem.

VALIDATING THE CLIENT

Conversing with clients has been discussed in terms of exploring the client's world and discovering possibilities for a better client future. The therapeutic conversation is also an interpersonal event that defines the relationship and forms the alliance. Inherent to the formation of a strong alliance is the validation of the client's experience. The objective of the validation process is to replace the invalidation that invariably accompanies veterans of impossibility to therapy. *The more impossible the problem, the more the need for the therapist to validate the client.*

Exploring the client's world and discovering possibilities makes the impossible possible. Validating the client makes the impossible probable. Validation requires the therapist to:

- legitimize the client's concerns.
- highlight the importance of the client's struggle with the problem and the problem itself.
- believe in the client and his or her abilities to resolve the problem.

Validation ensures a positive client experience of therapy, helps develop a strong alliance, and keeps therapy in tune with the client's theory of change. Validation also emphasizes the aspect of the therapeutic bond that has been most studied, namely therapist affirmation.

Affirmation is defined as acceptance, nonpossessive warmth, or positive regard. Orlinsky et al. (1994) reviewed 90 findings that indicate that the client's perception of therapist affirmation is a significant factor in promoting a positive outcome. Clients want to be liked and not condemned for their problems.

Validation begins simply by listening and allowing clients to tell their stories. The telling of the story is itself a powerful validation when told to an empathic and accepting listener. Clients hear their own voices and find validation in doing so (Parry, 1991).

Validation continues when the client's thoughts, feelings, and behaviors are accepted, believed, and considered completely understandable and justified. We genuinely hold the attitude that clients are doing their best under difficult circumstances.

As illustrated in the chapters that follow, validation sometimes includes respecting the validity of unusual ideas and behaviors. Validation does not constrain you to believe the client's story as the only possible explanation of the situation, but it does require that you not discount it. To illustrate, a client may come to your office and voice intense worry that the office is bugged by his enemies. Asking him to join you in searching the office for any listening devices would then be a concrete act of validation. Sweeping the office for "bugs" says to the client that his anxiety makes complete sense given his present experience of the world. No attempt is made to argue away his reality or brand it as crazy. It is taken at face value. Therapists need not be reality police, especially if there is a desire for success.

Validation of even bizarre perspectives opens the door for the therapist and the client to generate new ideas and directions. Validation of the existing frame of reference allows flexibility of that frame of reference. After realizing that there is no need to defend or argue the validity of a position or "delusion," clients often let go of the aspects of their beliefs that are not helpful. Validation allows people comfort and space to find face-saving ways out of their dilemmas.

Consider the invalidation that accompanied Katherine to therapy. Others' descriptions of her, as well as her own, were often indictments of her incompetence at relationships. Frequently criticized and made fun of, her concerns were not only discounted, but were also openly discredited as having no basis in reality. Her in-laws could say anything to her and not take responsibility for it because if she became upset, it wasn't at what they said, it was her problem of misinterpretation or oversensitivity. When she blew up in response, it wasn't because they were unkind, it was because she was a mental case.

This situation was worsened by the previous therapy's focus on the problem within her, reinforcing everyone's view of her incompetence. In the new therapy, Katherine found validation of her experience with her in-laws that replaced the invalidation of others (you're overreacting, you're "mental," you have confused boundaries and a poor sense of self) and her own invalidations (I'm incompetent at relationships). Validation of Katherine's belief that she was her in-law's resident scapegoat helped Katherine to address what she could do differently to tackle her in-laws.

Validation incorporates all aspects of the therapeutic process, from exploring the client's world to cocreating inventions. Both inventions codesigned for Katherine's encounters with her in-laws legitimized her belief that it was her in-laws' view of her that needed to change.

Katherine gave an Academy Award winning performance of Hepburn when her in-laws visited. She had fun with them for the first time. By the end of the weekend, she found herself joking and enjoying herself without playing a role. She particularly relished the dazed and confused look of her brother-in-law when she agreed with and exaggerated his comments about her therapy.

Discussion continued and Katherine noted more and more exceptions to her incompetence until she concluded that it never really existed, except with people who seemed to view her that way anyway. Katherine terminated therapy and returned to school to pursue her career as a teacher.

Validation builds a solid alliance, and sets the stage for client change. Many times, validation is all that is required to enable veterans of chronic invalidation to resolve their difficulties. Consider one final example that illustrates our belief that the more impossible a case appears, the greater the need to validate the client.

Erica, a mental health technician, was self-referred after her therapist of several years "downsized" his caseload. Erica's life was a tragic one in many respects. She endured several incidents of sexual abuse, spousal abuse, and had just completed treatment for cancer. Erica had been in therapy most of her life and had been hospitalized several times for suicide attempts. During the most recent hospitalization, Erica attempted suicide by hanging and narrowly escaped with her life. She was diagnosed borderline.

Perhaps representing the quintessential example of invalidation, Erica had recently begun experiencing a variety of physical symptoms, which she believed to be multiple sclerosis (MS). As though experiencing vision problems, extreme fatigue, and incontinence weren't bad enough, no one believed her!

Her family physician had examined her and referred her to a neurologist, who conducted a variety of tests to confirm the presence of MS. When the tests revealed no conclusive signs of MS, the family doctor and the neurologist conferred with her psychiatrist to discuss Erica's extensive mental health history. The conclusion was reached that the MS was a psychogenic reaction to the abandonment by her long-time therapist.

This interpretation was the final blow to Erica. Unfortunately, she concluded that maybe they were right. Maybe it was all in her head. After all, she was diagnosed borderline.

The therapist, accommodating Erica's familiarity with psychiatric diagnoses, suggested that Erica did not fit a profile of an individual who would "convert" psychological difficulties into physical problems, especially since such individuals tended to be psychologically unsophisticated, uneducated, and unaware of their mental distress. Erica of course was none of those and understood and experienced her psychic pain all too well, so well that she would at times cut herself to lesson the emotional pain.

The therapist also said that Erica did not fit factitious disorder either. *DSM-IV* (American Psychiatric Association, 1994) states that "the motivation for the behavior is to assume the sick role." Anyone having a discussion with Erica for five minutes could easily see that she was not motivated to assume a sick role. Quite the contrary. Erica hated the sick role and fought hard to separate any problems she had from her professional life. Erica's only refuge from her tragic life was her career and her view of herself as a professional helper. Furthermore, she had ample opportunity to assume a sick role when she was diagnosed with cancer. Instead, she battled the cancer, recovered from the surgery, and went back to work.

The conversation progressed to challenging the conclusion that her symptoms were psychogenic. They could not be psychogenic because Erica didn't fit a conversion or factitious disorder profile. Even Erica would have to agree that she was psychologically sophisticated and insightful, acutely aware of her own pain, and obviously invested in her career as a helper. Erica did agree.

She returned in the next session with a written description of a new diagnostic category named after her new therapist. Erica jokingly described a new factitious disorder that specifically feigned MS, and was motivated by an intense desire to assume a professional role. In this disorder, Erica continued, reaction formation is the primary defense. Erica laughed as she said that her intense drive to succeed, to overcome cancer, abuse, and the rest, were really equally intense calls to be cared for. Down deep, really deep, she actually did long for the sick role. Treatment recommendations, according to Erica, for the new disorder were lifelong extensive and expensive psychotherapy with its discoverer, or euthanasia by Kevorkian.

By the time the giggling stopped, Erica neither looked defeated nor acted demoralized. The therapist validated her position in a variety of ways and replaced the invalidation that others had implied or stated. Erica asked her family doctor for another neurological referral and warned him of legal recourse if he shared her mental health history.

The new neurologist diagnosed MS, first by the symptoms, and ultimately through opthamological tests. Erica was vindicated. While obviously a diagnosis of MS was a mixed blessing, Erica learned she could trust her feelings and judgment. Although therapy did not end at this point, and a few suicidal storms were weathered, the validation of Erica seemed to provide what she needed to pull her life together. The following are Erica's comments about therapy, written nearly a year later:

Looking back . . . it was your believing in me, that I was a person and not a patient. That's what our therapy was all about, wasn't it? Not a patient or a victim, but a person with potential and worth. It's what kept me alive.

Table 1
EXPLORING, DISCOVERING, AND VALIDATING: A SUMMARY

EXPLORING
Goals:
- To enlist client participation
- To ensure client's positive experience of the alliance
- To learn client's theory of change

Accomplished by:
- viewing client as healthy, capable, and competent
- depending on client's resources and ideas
- making client's input central
- being likable, friendly, and responsive
- making sure client feels understood
- being flexible and multidimensional
- thinking of oneself as an alien seeking a pristine understanding of client
- commiting to client's desires for treatment

DISCOVERING POSSIBILITIES
Goal:
- To identify exceptions, solutions, connections, and/or conclusions that permit a course of action, or render the problem no longer a problem

Accomplished by:
- accommodating client's theory of change
- being change-focused
- amplifying what works, avoiding what doesn't
- defining a changeable problem
- creating revision opportunities through conversation

VALIDATION
Goal:
- To replace the invalidation that accompanies veterans

Accomplished by:
- legitimizing client's concerns
- highlighting the importance of client's struggles
- believing in client and in his or her abilities
- accepting client at face value; avoiding role of reality police officer

You never sat in judgment or even as a "Doctor"—I never thought of you in that role. You walked with me and helped me untangle the knots, helped me see that I was capable of becoming who I wanted to become, not who anyone thought I should be. You helped me find my own way by being there for me, hearing me, believing me, and caring about me.

Looking beyond labels and giving clients the benefit of a doubt is critical with psychotherapy veterans. Behind every label used as explanation lies an invalidation. Chronic invalidations characterize impossibility. Replace that history with a competing experience of acceptance and validation and watch what clients can really do.

Table 1 provides a summary of exploring, discovering, and validating, which will be illustrated further in the next chapter.

CHAPTER 5

Exploring, Discovering, and Validating: The Case of Natalie

The foolish reject what they see, not what they think; the wise reject what they think, not what they see.

Huang Po

To illustrate exploring, discovering, and validating with an impossible case, the following edited transcript of excerpts from the first two sessions is presented with periodic commentary. How to accommodate therapist activities to the client's theory is illustrated through a most remarkable veteran of impossibility. This chapter introduces Natalie, who is diagnosed as having dissociative identity disorder. Natalie provides a provocative illustration of a well-developed theory of change. The dialogue brings to life the methods of exploring, discovering, and validating, and details her pathways to impossibility. Natalie's treatment concludes in Chapter 6.

Natalie was referred by her family physician, and identified herself as a multiple when scheduling the first appointment. She also indicated that she had just terminated with another therapist.

SESSION ONE

Excerpt One

T: So what led you to make an appointment with me?

C: We need some help. We've got some stuff going on that I've no idea what it is or why, and we're not real happy about it.

T: Okay, and what kind of trouble are you having?

C: I think there is some integration going on and it feels really weird. Some people that I'm used to talking to are not there.

T: Okay. So, that's pretty scary when you talk to them and they're not there.

C: We didn't really want to integrate. We were hoping just for, I believe they call it co-consciousness [starts to cry]. And I hate crying, especially my first visit.

T: That's okay. It's pretty frightening.

C: What do you need to know that will help?

T: There's so much that you know that I don't, that just about anything that you tell me is helpful for me to hear, but what I am most interested in knowing about is what you find distressing about the way things are now for you, so that we can work on that, because I don't have a preconceived notion about what needs to happen for you.

C: [Sighs] Thank you. Most everyone has. And that's been the hardest. Everyone has had preconceived notions and it's like we fit one person's definition over here and then on other parts, we didn't fit it at all, so they didn't like that. Well I can't help that.

Commentary

After the initial phone call from Natalie, the therapist was apprehensive. Visions of Sybil and Eve (attribution creep), and a skeptical attitude about therapist-created multiples or dissimulation (theory countertransference) combined to a strong need for the therapist to "take his own pulse" and "cultivate a beginner's mind." The therapist took the anxiety as a cue to discuss the case with colleagues. Consulting with colleagues enabled the therapist to start fresh, focus on listening to the client, and search for possibilities. The comment about preconceived notions was as much the therapist reminding himself as anything else.

The client's strong response to that early comment is perhaps reflective of her negative experience in therapy as well as her desire for validation. The therapist takes the client's comment as an encouragement to continue in the same vein.

Excerpt Two

T: When someone carries a particular diagnosis, that doesn't really tell me what the person wants, and that's what I'm interested in, what's best for you, and my job is to help you get to where you want to be, not to impose any framework on you as to where you should be on this, because if you are comfortable or accepting of yourself and there is just one aspect of that or a couple of aspects that are distressing, that's fine.

C: We are comfortable with it because some of us had different skills and it was like who was best able to handle the situation was there.

T: Umhm. What a wonderful system.

C: Well it was for us. I know it sounds crazy.

T: Doesn't sound crazy to me at all. It sounds very practical. You drew upon the different personalities in you that had the strengths to handle the situation you were in.

C: Yeah, that's what we'd done and then when we started, I guess, serious therapy, during this last year there's been a serious breakdown and we don't like it. It's scary. It's frightening and we were told, "Oh no, you're on the right process. You're integrating." I'm not so sure it's so great. I don't like it. I don't know what's happening that's causing that. I don't know if there's just been so much stress that we've just gone phft. That's I think maybe my biggest fear, if there is a breakdown. But I don't know where it is or what.

T: Okay. It sounds like the other therapist was attempting to break things down and integrate them.

C: She was. She was working with us and she said it was real important to identify the system and she wanted access to all the different alters.

Commentary

Note the pitfalls of theory countertransference (TC) and inattention to motivation in this case. The previous therapy dictated not only what to do (break down the system so integration could occur), but also how to do it (have each alter come out and talk). The prior therapy, from a theory-driven position, sent Natalie on the journey of breaking down the alters. Just like Molly, Natalie did not appreciate being told what to do and having her beliefs ignored. Natalie's motivation was clearly not in the direction of integration as the previous therapy defined it.

Excerpt Three

C: Well, perversely, the very fact that she seemed to think that was so very important made us very defensive. We've had too many people do things to us without our control and consent, and her seeming insistence on having access to call out . . . that just didn't sit right and it still doesn't.

T: Okay. It's really imposing.

C: Chris had the most apt description. She said, "It was like being asked to perform upon demand."

T: Okay.

C: And that just doesn't cut it [slight laugh].

T: Yeah.

C: Um, but in talking to Dr. R [referring physician] and amongst ourselves, she said you had a unique way of looking at the world and she felt that you would be willing to listen and that's enough for us.

Commentary

Natalie makes it clear what she is looking for from therapy: She wants to be listened to without being cubby-holed into the preconceived notions of attribution creep and theory countertransference. In retrospect, it may be surprising to fathom how listening to a client could represent such a difficult request. It is difficult because of the conventions borne in our training. TC and attribution creep are powerful influences. They are the culprits of impossibility.

Recall the outcome literature, the alliance research, and the importance of client perceptions of the relationship to a favorable outcome. Natalie felt intruded and imposed upon in her previous attempt at therapy, not a likely prerequisite for success. After cultivating a beginner's mind and assuming that therapy has not previously addressed the client's desires, the first step to clearing a path out of impossibility is shifting Natalie's negative experience of therapy, which has already started.

Excerpt Four

T: Okay, okay, I appreciate her confidence.

C: Being called to perform on demand is just, we just can't do it. See that's the other thing that we have found is that we don't quite have control of who comes and goes, but what we do know is that depending on what needed to be done, that person's there.

T: Uh-huh, uh-huh. I think that's wonderfully practical. I love practicality.

C: I mean that's where we've been and we're having problems because that's not occurring right now.

T: Okay, you're looking for the right person to come out, but yet that person's not there to access.

C: Not right there.

T: Okay. That is scary because that's how you've operated successfully for a long, long time.

C: But, we are experiencing breakdown and it's got to stop, or something has got to change. Normally, there is a three-year-old, that's Teresa. Linda is somewhere around eight or nine. Ah, there is Nancy, who is around fourteen, then the rest of us as those call us, the big girls. Um, there's me, I'm Nat, there's Gretchen, and there's Kerna, Chris, and Mary. And I can tell you what normally occurs for us. I have the greatest physical limitations where I have great difficulty handling stairs, I have great difficulty with things with balance, Gretchen runs up stairs, jumps, doesn't think a lick about it, you know, that is neat. And Chris is extremely articulate, extremely logical. She, she is our writer if you would.

T: Um, umhm.

C: When we've had to do business memos, communiqués, technical manuals, she's the writer. Gretchen is the mathematician and systems person. I am extremely intuitive. I know that might all sound crazy too, but I get little warning bells and when I don't pay attention to them we pay for it. And I've been that way for as long as I can remember . . . I mean even little. I always knew when it was safe to go home and my dad would be passed out so he couldn't get to us. I always knew, I mean I could be anywhere and I would know when it was safe to go home and I'd make sure we couldn't get home until that point as much as possible. Sometimes it would be beyond our control, but I always knew. I can walk into a room and I can kinda tell you who's mad at who, and who's interested in who, and I know that sounds crazy but they have relied on me for that.

T: Okay.

C: I've even, before the phone rang, knew who it was. I now if it's Mom, I know if it's Joe, and a couple of other close people, or I know it's someone I don't want to talk to [laughs]. That's terrible.

T: [Laughs]

C: So I just don't pick up the phone.

T: That sounds like a wonderful skill to have to me [laughs].

C: [Laughs] But I know that sounds bizarre and the therapists, they seem to have trouble believing that.

T: That's too bad.

C: And that's part of me, I think that's helped us survive some things.

T: Umhm, sounds like you didn't have a very good experience with therapy. You didn't feel like you were believed.

C: We weren't believed half the time, but we were trying anyway.

Commentary

"We weren't believed half the time, but we were trying anyway." That says it all. At times, clients whose stories are unconventional and different from normal middle class experience find themselves disbelieved and discredited. The incredible thing about her comment was the latter part—"but we're trying anyway"—an impressive demonstration of perseverance. Flying in the face of imposing frameworks, intrusive curiosity, disbelieving eyes, and total invalidation, Natalie continued in therapy in hopes of things improving. Replacing

Natalie's previously negative experiences in therapy with a validating context paved the way for a favorable conclusion.

The client's rapid, positive response to the therapist's comment about preconceived notions provided a good start for the client to perceive the therapeutic relationship favorably. Exploration also allowed a crystal clear client goal to emerge, namely, the restoration of access to her multiple personality system.

At this point the therapist was taking his own pulse. Although he felt positive about the session, nothing quickly came to mind regarding helping the client gain reaccess to her multiple system. The therapist knew he would be meeting with colleagues, and gave himself permission not to know what to do. He also reminded himself of his faith in the client and his confidence in the therapeutic process. This reminder has always served him well.

The therapist continues to explore, validating along the way, seeking possibilities for change.

Excerpt Five

T: [Sighs] Boy, I can see why you're really upset. What had been there before for you to draw upon, you're having trouble accessing it now. When did the breakdown start happening to you?

C: Okay, It's been just intermittent since some time around October, not anything that really bothered us. We figured we're just real tired. We have Epstein-Barr. That does affect us across the board in different ways. But we've noticed a lot really getting bad since about January. It's been since Joe [her boyfriend] started his stuff he has been going through. His father just died and there is a big inheritance fight with his brother and sister. He is really a basket case and has been explosive, like a time bomb waiting to explode. Joe, one time, threatened to kill them both! It's one blow-up after another.

Commentary

A possibility is discovered. The client connects her difficulties in accessing to her current volatile situation with her live-in boyfriend,

Joe. While it is unknown whether this opportunity will allow for solutions to the accessing problem, it does represent a clear connection to a difficulty that can be addressed in therapy. The therapist files this possibility and continues to explore the client's system of accessing her alters, attempting to understand her unique way of negotiating the world.

Excerpt Six

T: The normal methods or ways of accessing are not working.

C: Right.

T: So, you will kinda go through the process you would normally go through.

C: Right, it was like they're not there.

T: And they're not there. It's like you would walk into the room and like Teresa wouldn't be there.

C: Yeah, she's not there, yeah.

T: Okay.

C: And like when I go looking, I can't find her.

T: Umhm.

C: And on their part, Nancy was out last night for a little while. She hasn't been able to find Chris. Chris always took care of them, always, because there were some times when dad would be doing things and Chris could hide them so they wouldn't have to deal with it.

T: Okay. I'm trying to understand your system. Through imagery, you have a house, a room system.

C: Yeah, I guess so. I guess so.

T: And you go from room to room to find your alters.

C: Yeah, and we have an outside area that you can play. I guess that sounds crazy, but it is.

T: It doesn't sound crazy to me. It sounds like a very efficient system.

C: Yeah, each one, it was decorated the way they liked it and . . . [starts crying again].

T: Okay.

C: And I'm tired of crying.

T: Well you have a major loss in your life. Hopefully this is not permanent.

C: I think that's what I'm afraid of and I don't know how on earth I will deal with things after this.

T: Whew, well, no, your method of coping would be gone.

C: It's just like it's gone kaput.

T: The stress that you're undergoing has been quite a load.

C: It has been substantial.

T: I mean with dealing with Joe and all of what he's gone through is also . . .

C: It's been hard.

T: It's been real hard, to the point where he has been threatening to kill his brother and sister. It may be that because this situation with Joe is a big-time stressor in your life, that it may not be that they are breaking down or integrating, but rather that they're not accessible, they are hiding.

C: Because it's too much?

T: Because it's too much. Because Joe's blow-ups are too much.

Commentary

The therapist returns to the possibility discovered earlier, the connection between the difficulty accessing her alters and the stressful situation with Joe. Through the exploration process, the therapist has entered the client's world and established her frame of reference as valid. Conversing within that world then allows the therapist to pose the possibility that the alters are not breaking down, but instead are inaccessible because of the stress of Joe's outbursts. Although not yet discussed, an implication is that if Joe's blow-ups are addressed or the resulting fear handled, then her access routes may reappear. It is near the end of the session, and the possibility has been planted. The therapist next asks the client to think about the ways she has previously gained access, thereby continuing to explore her world and additional possibilities for a better future.

Excerpt Seven

T: If you think it's a good idea, I would suggest that you think of all the ways you have gained access before.

C: That's a good idea. I'm open. And it is just whoever handled it, well, they knew what to do.

T: Whoever had the best skills in that area. That's a wonderful system.

C: Yes, that's what we did. Thank you. God bless your heart. You are literally the first person who has ever said that. You are the first and everyone else is telling us, "You are wrong. You are messed up. You have to do this," and we were literally, all of us have sat there and said, "I don't think we're so bad."

T: Umhm, umhm, good for you because you're not.

C: But we did want co-consciousness. That is what we were always hoping for.

T: Umhm, it makes a lot of sense.

C: We have had successful jobs. Our art work is showing. We won awards. That kind of stuff wouldn't have happened if we had been so dysfunctional.

T: That's right.

C: Now, we're dysfunctional.

T: Because you can't have access to all of your resources, all of the people who have been helpful to you.

Commentary

The session ends on a very positive note, "You are the first . . . " The goals of exploring the client's world have been met. The client openly participated and reported a promising view of therapy. In addition, a possibility for change had been discovered. If the situation with Joe could be managed better, perhaps then the access route would return to her alters. The therapist legitimized the client's concerns, highlighted their importance, and believed in the client. After the first session, the therapist felt that change was not only possible, but probable. The therapist felt positive even though he didn't have any concrete plan about how the client could regain access. The therapist maintained his faith in the client and faith in the process.

A team of colleagues met and watched the videotape of the first session. Watching the tape and the ensuing discussion helped the therapist stay focused on the client and what she was asking for from treatment. The overwhelming message from the team was for the therapist to "go slow" and keep doing what he was doing: listening, validating, avoiding attribution creep and TC. The team felt that the process looked very hopeful.

SESSION TWO

Excerpt One

T: So, how are you doing?

C: Well it's a little bit of a difficult answer, ahm, I'm a bit, a bit at a loss, I'm Chris.

T: All right.

C: And, Nat's journals were not too good, but I got pretty much of the gist of what had been going on and I find that I am extremely angry. The weekend was quite a harrowing weekend because Joe was bound and determined to go see his daughter and Nat has been telling him that it was not a good idea. She had a bad feeling about it and he could at least delay it one week. Well it was totally out of the question so we ended up going and we were in the middle of the blizzard and I am absolutely fed up with self-destructive behavior. I mean no matter what anyone said it did not get through to him.

T: Umhm, umhm.

C: And I'm sick of it. I'd like to tell him to get a grip on reality, but coming from a multiple that's kind of humorous in itself. [Both laugh]

T: What are you angry about?

C: I guess where I am coming from is, on the first side to be fair to him, he has brought a lot of good things into our lives, but the last eight to ten weeks have been absolute hell. It has been to the point where we don't even want to come home because we don't know what we're going to be encountering. I am a pretty direct communicator. Nat and Gretchen are more indirect, a little bit softer.

T: All right, uh-huh.

C: And they have expressed they're uncomfortable with the intensity and the uncontrollableness of him and his behavior and with his anger. It just kept getting worse. His blow-ups are intolerable. And then the trip over the weekend was really rough. He was just maniacal and doing some stupid actions and I am actually aching from the stress of all that. Actually physically aching.

T: Okay.

C: And I'm angry about that too.

T: Umhm.

C: I can't reach the little ones and I've always taken care of them. So I don't know what to tell you. Nat has been trying, as you had asked her to try, to be conscious of how she has accessed in the past.

T: Umhm, umhm.

C: And she journaled that, so if any of us would happen to come out, we would see it. She put it in a very prominent place so we can't miss it.

T: Okay, terrific.

C: And she went back to the old system that we had, we always had one pad in one place. And we log and we read.

T: Okay, good. Is it allowing access to the different people?

C: Not real well, I can't reach the little ones. I am worried about that.

T: Okay.

C: I think frankly, they're hiding and I don't blame them.

T: I don't know if Nat was able to journal this to you, one thing that we kicked around the last time was that this whole thing with Joe and all this stress is making everyone retreat to their areas of comfort, and that's what is making it difficult to access them.

C: I think so, and I am angry at him for that.

T: Umhm.

C: I have tried expressing that to him.

T: Umhm.

C: And he, for whatever reason, does not want to hear it.

T: Umhm.

Commentary

A different personality attends session two and the therapist is eager to gain her perspective of the situation. Chris expands the conversation and gives more detail about the situation with Joe. She expresses her anger as the therapist explores her story, searching for possibilities and the opportunity to follow-up on the previous session's discovery. The opportunity occurs and the connection remains intact, and even appears stronger given the client's remark, "they're hiding and I don't blame them."

The therapist continues to learn the client's theory and explores her attempts with old methods of accessing her personalities. The client's world continues to unfold as the therapist asks further questions about her accessing system and Joe's blow-ups.

Excerpt Two

C: It's not working very well. I'm lucky to have been able to get out.

T: When you told me that you were Chris, the first thing that came to my mind was, "How did you get out? How did it happen?"

C: Honest to God, I don't know.

T: Okay.

C: It is like I woke up two days ago, I'm the one who woke up.

T: Okay.

C: I can't reach the little ones. That disturbs me greatly.

T: Umhm.

C: Because I would always go play with them. I taught them to read. I always let them know when it was okay to be out, and they could have their play time.

T: Umhm.

C: I was the one who made sure they knew when the big girls had to work.

T: Umhm, umhm.

C: I can't reach 'em.

T: Okay.

C: Normally, Gretchen has a house. I can't find the path to her house anymore. I mean it was a well-beaten path.

T: Was it an image that you would utilize to access Gretchen? Or— I'm trying to make this concrete.

C: Oh, I don't mind. I don't know how to answer you because I could close my eyes and I would walk down that path and here I'd be.

T: Okay.

C: And sometimes I didn't even have to do that.

T: Umhm, umhm. But that was one method; certainly that was a successful one.

C: Yes.

T: Ahm, that's not working for you now.

C: No, I mean the path is gone.

T: Okay.

C: I guess this probably sounds kinda bizarre but we all have our own place to be, they're all decorated. They're all things reflecting their own taste. But it's all gone now. I can't find the little ones.

T: Do you think that if the stress of this situation was reduced that they would become accessible?

C: I've been asking that and, actually I thought about that, and yes I think so.

T: Okay.

C: I was trying to figure that out, because I was trying to remember when things would be really bad with dad, what would happen. With dad though, I would get the little ones and I would make sure they were hidden so they wouldn't have to see and they wouldn't have to hear.

T: Umhm.

C: And then Kerna was the best physical fighter. My dad tried to kill my brother a couple of times. Kerna stopped him one time. He had a hatchet in his hand and was after him and Kerna stopped him. And so, depending on the situation, ahm, Kerna was the best physical fighter.

T: That's really the beauty of the system. It's that you have been able to access the best in a given situation to deal with what's happening. That's the beauty of your system.

C: Yes, I didn't think we were so bad.

T: Yeah, I don't think you're so bad at all. It's bad that you're having difficulty accessing someone when it has always worked for you.

C: Yes, that's bad for us.

T: Definitely.

C: I have just been astounded at how much we have been ostracized since word of this got around. One person said Satan is involved in this and you need to be exorcised and you need to go get fixed. I wanted to go, "Boogie, boogie, boogie," and chase her down the hall. [Both laugh]

T: It would have been kinda fun to do that. The lack of acceptance is not only among lay people but it's just as rampant among professionals.

C: You are the first, Nat came home and told us, and I'm grateful. She said you gave her hope. The other doctors we have seen treated us like we were something from a freak show. One person wanted access on demand. Excuse me! Who the hell are you?

T: Really, that's pretty intrusive.

C: I thought so.

T: Yeah, not very respectful.

C: And I also found that frankly, after what has been done to us by our dad, that was just as obnoxious. And everywhere we were getting, "Oh, this is bad, you're bad. This is wrong. You need to integrate." We didn't want to integrate. What we do want is co-consciousness. That would make life easier. Nancy asked our last doctor, Nancy was out and she was crying and she said, "Am I going to go away?" And the doctor couldn't tell her yes, no, maybe. That's not acceptable.

T: No, umhm.

C: And that's not acceptable to us as the big girls.

T: Why would you want them to go away?

C: We don't. Thank you for giving us, I wanted to tell you, thank you for giving us hope. Because you are the first one who said, "No you really are not so bad."

T: Yes. I think you're more than not so bad.

C: Well right now it doesn't feel like it.

T: This is a major stressor you're experiencing now and the person that is the most significant person in your life right now has been unreasonable and unkind to you in a lot of ways and is, is going down a completely unproductive path, incredible upheaval. And despite all your efforts to try to be helpful to him, he has been like a pit viper to you.

C: Yes.

T: He goes off on these very unproductive blow-ups and self-defeating things, and you see that so readily, you want to talk him out of that, and that's not getting you anywhere.

C: No.

T: The other part of it is that if that situation is addressed and it becomes less stressful and you become less frightened, your access paths to all of you will then be there. I think that's kind of our working hypothesis.

C: That's what it feels like.

T: Okay, okay.

C: That's what it feels like.

T: I think we're in sync there, so if we address that issue then access may redevelop for you, the way that it should be and always worked well for you before.

DISCUSSION

The discovery process is complete. A possibility emerged that could permit a solution to the accessing problem. The client's presentation of her concerns was successfully connected to a description of the problem that could promote change. The implication evolved that the alters were inaccessible, not because they were breaking down, but because they had retreated to their areas of comfort. They were hiding from Joe's emotional storms and self-destructive behaviors. The alters were protecting themselves.

The therapist asked the client if she thought that addressing the Joe situation would allow her access to return. She replied affirmatively. The therapist and client agreed upon the problem and mutually formulated how the problem could be addressed by altering the situation with Joe. The alliance, therefore, appeared to be strong.

Many opportunities for continuing validation arose and the therapist responded several times in ways that legitimized and highlighted the client's theory. The client responded by saying that she was grateful that the therapist had given them hope. Many clients report that the instillation of hope is a potent curative factor in therapy (Frank & Frank, 1991; Murphy, Cramer, & Lillie, 1984).

The stage is now set. Exploring, discovering, and validating have opened a pathway for Natalie out of her dilemma and, as we see in Chapter 6, to much more.

SECTION III

CLINICAL APPLICATIONS

Success is counted sweetest
By those who ne'er succeed.
To comprehend a nectar
Requires sorest need.

Not one of all the purple host
who took the flag today
Can tell the definition,
So clear, of victory,

As he, defeated, dying,
On whose forbidden ear
The distant strains of triumph
Break, agonized and clear.

Emily Dickinson

Case Example: Dissociative Identity Disorder or "A Collage of Gifts"

That so few dare to be eccentric marks the chief danger of the time.

John Stuart Mill

THIS CHAPTER FOLLOWS and concludes Natalie's therapy, detailing the concrete clinical methodology of working with battle-weary veterans of failed psychotherapy. The chapter begins with a brief survey of the current views regarding this disorder and the prevailing methods of treatment. We then follow with Natalie's experience in therapy, inviting the reader to compare and contrast.

Through the use of excerpted transcripts, we carefully trace the process of change. Within a short period, accommodating the client's frame of reference and honoring her theory of change pays off with big dividends.

DISSOCIATION DISORDER: TREATMENT RECOMMENDATIONS

Overview

The history of psychotherapy suggests that as much as therapies are moved by the forces of fashion, so too are diagnoses. One of the latest to achieve preeminence or elite status is dissociative identity disorder (DID), previously known as multiple personality disorder.

91

Perhaps more than any other condition in recent memory, DID has spurred considerable controversy, particularly over its very existence. Once seen as exceedingly rare (Meyer & Salmon, 1988), it now is regarded as afflicting one to three percent of the population (Lowenstein, 1992).

Defining what DID is *not* is perhaps easier than defining what it is. It is accepted that the condition is not a schizophrenia. Clients, it is said, do not show the kinds of disturbances of cognition and affect associated with a psychotic level of disturbance, although psychotic-like experiences, including auditory hallucinations and thought insertion and withdrawal, may present. The personality structure is one based on dissociation and posttraumatic factors, not borderline or psychotic ego organization. Clients with the condition are also described as capable of object relatedness. That is, they are warm and self-observant in contrast to the internal experience of emptiness, even deadness, associated with borderline and psychotic individuals (Lowenstein, 1992).

The classic clinical manifestation of DID is the client's alternation among two or more distinct personalities (Cavenar, Jr., & Brodie, 1983). These personalities are often called alters or entities. Lowenstein (1992) writes that the alters for most DID clients are not highly elaborated and possess a limited range of thoughts, affects, and associated behaviors. The alters are also mercurial in that they may overlap, interfere with each other, and appear simultaneously. Lowenstein adds that fully formed alters do not always switch and transfer executive control of the person. To make the diagnosis, the latest DSM criteria require that some form of amnesia or blank spell must be experienced.

Treatment

As with many conditions, the treatment of DID is based more on conjecture and clinical judgment than empirically validated protocols. Individual, group, inpatient, pharmacologic, and other approaches are recommended with no substantial support other than the unrestrained enthusiasm of their advocates. Complicating the job for practicing clinicians is that data on long-term follow up are largely nonexistent. Inasmuch as follow-up data are missing, so too are comparative treatment outcome studies (Dunn, 1992).

Yet, as with borderline clients, the principal treatment is some form of individual therapy. The therapist's charge is to integrate the memories, feelings, and cognitive distortions related to the precipitating trauma. The therapy is also intended to help the client replace dissociative defenses with other ones less disruptive to healthy functioning (Lowenstein, 1992).

Nemiah (1989) writes that the clinician should take steps to explore actively the dissociated personalities, encourage them to become aware of one another across amnestic barriers, and facilitate a catharsis of the traumatic memories, especially those associated with child abuse. In this work of uncovering, Nemiah warns of challenge and periods of anxiety for both treater and client, especially "when aggressive or suicidal personalities are in the ascendancy" (p. 1038). It is at these more troublesome times that brief hospitalization may be necessary to lend support.

Lowenstein (1992) asks that the treatment of DID be understood as classical ego-psychologically oriented psychotherapy. In this context, the client's alters can be viewed as concretized or personified free associations; no alter should be excluded. He further recommends that any work on the genetic roots of symptoms be postponed until the client's defenses are up to the task. The clue to improved defensive functioning is that the alters work together more effectively. In his opinion, clients who are engaged in a psychotherapy designed or constructed to deal with the DID can have a good outcome, including full resolution of the multiplicity.

Summary

Conclusions regarding the status of the DID diagnosis, much less its treatment, are difficult to make. Kluft (1991a) describes the current state of the art as preliminary, but at the same time suggests that DID be included in all differential diagnoses (Kluft, 1991b)—a curious position. Suffice it to say that at this stage, all treatments of DID are at best experimental and unproven. Any doctrinaire claims of the value and effectiveness of any therapy for DID should be viewed as suspect.

The putative tradition for the treatment of DID emphasizes the idea of integration. Namely, as dissociation is seen as somehow fracturing the continuity of the client's mental life, integrating the alters will perforce be curative.

THE CASE OF NATALIE

Remember that Natalie, diagnosed with dissociative disorder, re-entered therapy because she had lost access to her alters. This was extremely distressing not only because Natalie relied on the different talents of the alters to function, but she also considered them like her family. Natalie defined success as restoration of her multiple system.

Exploring Natalie's world led to the discussion of her live-in boy-friend Joe's recent traumas and his propensity to blow up in fits of anger. The connection emerged that the difficulty accessing was caused by the stress and fear associated with dealing with Joe's erratic behavior. Natalie's theory of change was that if the situation with Joe was addressed and the stress reduced, her access would return.

SESSION THREE

Excerpt One

T: So, how are things? The accessing problem, dealing with Joe's blow-ups, and also the hypothesis we were developing that if you were able to have some inroads to deal with Joe, you wouldn't be as frightened, and perhaps be able to gain access again.

C: Well, I think we had a total breakdown, because during this past weekend Joe was in a real foul mood one day and he just really exploded. Boy this is really hard because it's like everything is so blurred. He had called his brother and sister. It was not a good phone call. He still doesn't realize the impact of his call. I don't see the point of going over it with him. He exploded because I told him I wished he had let me know he had called because I would have handled the call differently. He had his temper tantrum and then, I was just really tired. It was like I didn't even have any energy and I went to bed and I called in Monday and I slept all day.

T: Umhm.

C: I just couldn't think. Tuesday I went into work a half day. I was real shaky. And then, Wednesday, I went to bed. We did not have a good Wednesday evening. He didn't want to hear anything, what we're angry or hurt about. He doesn't want to hear why we're upset. He doesn't want to hear it [emphatically]!

T: Umhm, umhm, that doesn't wash very well.

C: No, and we don't think he even realizes it and I don't feel very good about that either. I think it stinks. And yet he says he's still excited by me. Oh yeah, whoopee. He thinks things can continue as normal. Well, no way.

T: Okay.

C: When we try to express it he really goes off the deep end and he told me I was being like his dad, repeatedly bringing things up and lambasting him with it. No I'm not, but I have the right to be heard.

T: Yes.

C: The one night when we tried to talk about it he said, "Well, I'm going to leave. I've had it." He said, "And when I leave I'm going to stuff a rag in the engine and blow it up." It's just too much. So I think we had a real breakdown and I'm numb. Yeah. We're seeing a very selfish person right now and it doesn't feel right.

T: Umhm.

C: I just don't think that Joe realizes how much of a negative impact it has been. And when I try to tell him that, he just doesn't want to hear it. And I don't understand that. And I'm not saying I'm perfect. That's asinine too, but, I don't see the point in trying anymore. It's like I can't get through to him. It's like he doesn't want to hear it [emphatically]. And I don't know what to do anymore because I'm tired.

T: So you're tired and withdrawing, escaping, and sleeping more and don't want to interact with him as much.

C: Yeah.

T: He's not noticing that?

C: No, and the Epstein-Barr is also very active right now and I don't think he realizes that. The Epstein-Barr is also impacting, but this situation with Joe is having a greater impact.

T: Umhm. One thing that certainly seems apparent is that he is not sensitive to the effect all this is having on you. Not sensitive enough that he can look beyond his own situation.

C: No.

T: Which makes you upset and likely resentful.

C: Yeah, I am resentful, real resentful.

T: Umhm.

C: And I don't know if I'm expecting too much.

T: I don't think that's expecting too much. Because a person is going through something that is rough for them does not give them justification for being totally insensitive to those around them. He's obviously having a rough time, but it's self-defeating to strike out at those that you care about the most.

C: Well, I kind of think so. At least that's what I've always thought. But I don't like this numbness, and I don't like this just wanting to go to bed. And I don't like things at work feeling overwhelming when I know it's normally what I can do in my sleep.

T: Umhm, okay.

C: But I think we had a breakdown.

T: Boy, it sounds like it's gotten real bad for you with Joe. You still have that whole process happening the way we have talked about it before, the first time with you, and the last time with Chris. There seems to be a pretty good relationship between what's going on with you and Joe and the problem you're having accessing.

C: I think so. I haven't been able to tell him that. The impact of his anger, because it's so forceful, it has really hit us hard and we don't have a way to deflect that.

T: Umhm.

C: And I tried telling him that before, and it's like it just doesn't get through. I don't know anymore what it will take to get through to him. I'm pretty sure that's why the little ones have hidden. Something in my gut tells me I think you're right, I think you're dead on! And [pause] I just don't know what to do.

Commentary

Nat attended session three and seemed hopeless about her situation with Joe. She felt as though she had experienced a total breakdown. The therapist stayed with her throughout the discussion, and validated her feelings of despair and resentment. The connection between the breakdown and Joe's behavior was stronger than ever, as evidenced by the client's "dead on" comment. Given that strong connection and Natalie's theory that her alters could be restored if the situation with Joe improved, the therapist was ready to introduce an idea for Nat's consideration. The therapist had already discussed the idea with a team of colleagues.

Presenting Ideas

In introducing ideas to clients, we keep three things in mind. First is the recognition that any idea depends upon the resources of the client for success. Therapist dependence accurately portrays the nature of change as therapist reliance on client resources and participation. Second is our explicit acceptance of what the client wants and a search for options that directly address the client's desires. *If an idea does not pass that acid test, then it is discarded.*

Finally, and perhaps most importantly, we rely on the client's positive reception to therapist ideas. If the client does not enthusiastically endorse the idea, it is abandoned. Options are discussed and openly evaluated. Reliance on a favorable response not only continues the client's intimate participation, but also enables the client to have ownership of the ideas. Ownership encourages clients to utilize their resources to resolve problems.

Natalie was angry with Joe and fed up with his explosive behavior. She perceived Joe as the problem. Exploration of Natalie's world not only revealed her theory of change, but also provided some direction for the invention process. Natalie's solutions largely revolved around unsuccessful attempts to be heard regarding Joe's negative impact on her. She repeatedly expressed her frustration about "not getting through." The combination of her resentment and her repetitive attempts to get through led to the following discussion of an idea to enable her to get her message across and regain access. Notice how the therapist's suggestion is accommodated to the client's language.

Excerpt Two

C: And [pause] I just don't know what to do.

T: Okay. Well, I had kind of a crazy thought about it, that I wanted to bounce off of you. It certainly doesn't fit everybody.

C: I've certainly heard a lot of strange things before, so have at it.

T: Okay, I thought you would be open to thinking about it, but it's one of those things that you like it or you don't. It's a more indirect way of approaching your breakdown and dealing with Joe and his anger, and the connection of those two. I was thinking about it before you said this word, but when you said the word "deflect," that made me think, I'm gonna bring it up. I agree, you need something to deflect that anger and the impact of that situation on you.

C: Yes.

T: And on your ability to access all of you. It's like they're frightened and they're hiding and, unless there's a way to deal with Joe and deflect that anger, they're not going to want to come back out. The way of deflecting I had in mind is called "constructive payback" and that pretty well describes what it is. It's for use in situations where directly trying to get through to another person is not hitting the mark. You've tried to tell Joe that you're affected by his blow-ups and that you're upset but he, for whatever reason, has stonewalled it. He's not able to take that in. He's not able to be sensitive to your pain so he essentially blows you off.

C: Yeah.

T: And feels quite justified in his own position without appreciating yours.

C: Yeah, exactly.

T: And you have responsibly tried to bring it to his attention, but yet he doesn't hear it. Chris did it directly, articulately, and you've done it in other ways, more compassionately. Neither of those methods of directness have hit the mark though.

C: No.

T: Constructive payback would entail that you make intentional mistakes that directly affect Joe in harmless but irritating ways. Your creativity will be a great help here, because it takes some creativity to figure out ways to apply this. Some examples, and these may not fit for you, people that prepare meals may over- or undercook food or put debris in the food, or vacuum when he's on the telephone or watching his favorite TV program, or blocking his car when he has to get somewhere in a hurry.

C: [Laughs] I see what it does. Indirectly, it's like we're continuing our life and our activity and we're not aware of the impact that it has on him.

T: Exactly. And when he says, "Gosh, what the heck is going on here?" You might say, "Boy, I haven't been myself lately. I don't know what's happening here. I've been so depressed and confused lately. I've just been making mistakes right and left." So rather than directly confronting him with it, you pay him back without taking ownership for it.

C: It will visibly show him what in the hell is going on.

T: Yes, exactly, without ever saying it directly. You are incredibly perceptive. Hopefully he'll notice that there's something wrong here. This is not usual behavior for you.

C: Yes, so he'll think "Why is this behavior occurring?"

T: Exactly. "Does it have anything to do with me being a jerk?" [Both laugh]

C: That'd probably be too easy to wish for. But it would start him asking why and usually if someone at least starts asking why, then—

T: Then they're not focused internally. They're focused on the other people.

C: That's right. They're starting to pay attention to the world again.

T: Exactly. The other thing that it may do is allow you to deflect his anger in a positive way that hopefully will result in you feeling less frightened.

C: Yes, it sounds great. The closest one who has ever done anything like that is Kerna. One time, we are very good dancers and we had a couple dance. There was this person who insisted on dancing with Kerna and kept grabbing her too tight and in the wrong places, so she began screaming at the top of her lungs, "Oh, my phalanges, my phalanges, you're killing my phalanges," and it just stopped everybody on the dance floor [both laugh]. And it embarrassed the poor guy to death, and he didn't show up for the rest of the evening.

T: [Laughs]

C: So I think the creativity is there. But yeah, that would definitely be out of character for us.

T: And if that'll confuse him that'll be great because—

C: And that'll stop that chain of reaction too.

T: Yes, yes exactly, it's a way of him interrupting. It's like if he's thinking about what's happening with you, he's not going to be embroiled in this process of nailing you.

C: I see. I see what you're thinking. I think that is a really neat idea. I really do.

T: Good. Good, because really when you said the word deflect it made me think of it. It really highlighted it for me.

C: And I think you're right. Oh, man. I have to laugh at it 'cause I really hope it'll do some of the things I'm hoping, and I also hope that it will act as an interrupt for our accessing problem.

Commentary

Constructive payback is based on the MRI technique of benevolent sabotage.* The client responded very favorably to the idea, immediately understanding it and expressing her personal explanation of its mechanism of action. Natalie also connected the idea to an incident in her past, an excellent indication of a complete match.

When we present an idea for consideration, we specifically observe the client's response. Cool or lukewarm responses are taken very seriously and are not pushed or pursued. We look for a full-blown positive response in which the client immediately reacts with an application strategy or connects the idea to something that is similar in their experience or explains the idea specifically applied to their lives.

Let's retrace the steps to this idea of constructive payback and account for Natalie's overwhelmingly favorable response. The thera-

*There are many explanations for its usefulness; please see Fisch et al. (1982) for a full explanation.

pist accepted the client's views of her situation and legitimized her understandable distress. Validation of Natalie's belief that it was okay to be a multiple, as well as her view that Joe's blow-ups were the major source of her accessing problem, helped her to address the situation with Joe. The therapist used the client's language as much as possible when he presented the idea.

Constructive payback legitimized and justified her belief that Joe and his anger were causing the breakdown. Each time she applied the technique with Joe, therefore, demonstrated the therapist's validation of Natalie's theory. The validation context was consequently extended outside the session to the client's social environment, encouraging her to use her resources to address the problem. Constructive payback emerged from Natalie's theory, depended on her creativity, addressed her goal for treatment, and was openly and collaboratively evaluated.

SESSION FOUR

Excerpt One

T: Have you had an opportunity to try any of the things that we've talked about?

C: Yeah [slight laugh] it was quite fun.

T: Good. I was hoping it would be.

C: Actually, we did not have to do many at all. Nat left a note for everybody and I would say a lot of things changed after that talk with you. That evening and that next day some different things were tried, and then that next evening Joe said, "Obviously something is wrong so what gives?" Chris was out and she told him. I think it's made a big difference because I'm out and Linda was out earlier in the week also.

T: Wonderful! I'm really glad to hear that. So who are you?

C: I'm Gretchen.

T: Hi, Gretchen. Well that's terrific.

C: I am much relieved. Because I couldn't find anybody. I couldn't reach anybody. So, I'm out for awhile. Nat and Chris can have a break. They need it.

T: That's great. I don't know if this got communicated to you, that one of the things that we talked about was that if the situation with Joe got handled then perhaps everyone wouldn't be so afraid, and your normal access paths would start opening up.

C: Yes, I think that's occurring. I have seen Nat and Chris. I've also gotten to see Nancy and that was a first for a long time too. So I would say something has changed.

T: Okay, and what would you say that is that has changed?

C: I think I would attribute it a lot to the relationship and this stress having been reduced with Joe.

T: Okay.

C: I really would. I'm not going to say it's roses but at least the element of thinking he's going to go off the deep end again has finally been eliminated and the element of his explosive violence seems to be restrained.

Commentary

Access is restored! Natalie implemented the technique and invented ways to apply it that fit her world and her experience. She used her unique resources to not only creatively discover imaginative ways to pay Joe back, but also to incorporate the technique into her multiple system. Once Joe asked the question and was at last ready to hear the answer, Chris was right there to set him straight. Constructive payback became far more than any technique could ever be: It became an invention, a personal discovery that allowed reaccess to occur. We doubt that the MRI had reaccess in mind when they developed the technique!

Despite Natalie's success, constructive payback is just a technique and, as such, has no intrinsic value apart from the client and the relationship. Technique is a behavioral manifestation of the relationship, and a measure of the client's perception of, and participation in, the therapeutic endeavor. A technique, regardless of its success in a particular case, is at most a helpful possibility for both therapist and client to consider. This is not to say that techniques are irrelevant, but that their power for change is not derived from any intrinsic, inherent, or invariant quality. It was Natalie's talents that empowered the idea, and her positive view of the relationship that imbued the technique with value.

Constructive payback accomplished everything that Natalie hoped it would. She regained access and finally got her message across to Joe. Now that the changes have occurred, the therapeutic task is to empower the changes.

Excerpt Two

T: Great, tell me what you did.

C: Kerna tried the vacuum trick while he was on the phone, and then another thing we did, our hearing is pretty sensitive so, we turned the answering machine way down [laughs]. And so he was always having to scramble to get the phone and when he was done on the phone, she would push it way down again [laughs]. Just real aggravating [laughs].

T: Umhm, umhm.

C: And every time he left his tea glass somewhere it would get picked up and dumped in the sink. [Both laugh]

T: So he'd come back and say, "Where's my tea?"

C: Yeah, yeah.

T: "I thought you were done with it" [laughs].

C: Yeah, and it worked. I can see how someone can have a lot of fun with that and I knew I could get a lot more creative, but you know that wasn't the point.

T: Umhm, right, it was to deflect a lot of that anger out and have some impact.

C: I think it did, because Chris told him and told him quite well.

T: What did Chris tell him?

C: That he had hurt us a lot. That we could not deal with the explosions any more.

T: Umhm.

C: And that got hashed out for a long time, for the first time.

T: Great. Do you think that the little things that you were doing, like the answering machine and the tea glass—

C: Yeah, definitely I think that really had an impact, because we were doing it deliberately.

T: So it had the impact of discharging some of your frustration and anger.

C: Yes. It was great. It was fun [laughs].

T: Then, did Joe ask you what was going on or—

C: He said, "Obviously something is really wrong." And he said, "I think I have been kind of bad for you," and Chris said, "Yes, you have."

T: Okay. Great! So he did focus outside onto you.

C: Yes, that is what happened and Chris said, "Yes, you were."

T: Tremendous! And Chris was right there ready to take over.

C: Yes.

T: That's wonderful.

C: Nat couldn't.

T: Well, that's not Nat's strength. It just seems that that's Chris's forte.

C: Yes it is.

T: Yes. And that's what's so wonderful about your system that the one who has the strength is the one who comes out.

C: Yeah, that has been our pattern all through our lives.

T: Umhm, and that's hard to argue with. That sounds so perfect to me.

C: I don't think we're so bad.

T: Well, I'm really glad that you're starting to be able to use all of you.

C: I am too.

T: Did Joe become aware that these things were intentionally done by you?

C: No, and we're never going to tell him.

T: Okay. Good, good [laughs]. Some things are better left unsaid.

C: It served the purpose, and it did us a lot of good too. 'Cause it was really nice to be able to annoy him just a little bit. It was a lot of fun. I could be a real prankster [both laugh]. I really could.

T: Umhm.

C: But I think it's okay because the point was to interrupt him and it did. It interrupted.

T: Umhm, and that was exactly the point.

C: And that was what Nat had said. She thought it would be something that would work and it did. So I think that actually we all want to say, "Thank you."

T: Oh, you're all really very welcome. The idea was a good one, but it took your creativity in application to make it happen. It seemed to fit for me to bring that up because of the way Nat was describing the situation, that she needed something and you all needed something to deflect it when he's like that and —

C: Yeah.

T: To have him interrupt the process and in the meantime get rid of some of that frustration and resentment that was building up.

C: Yeah, because there was a lot of resentment.

T: And that was getting in the way of accessing. The resentment combined with being frightened was blocking access.

C: It was a nasty, nasty combination.

T: But you've taken that situation and have worked it through.

C: Right.

T: And what seemed to be the kick-off to all that, was when you heard Chris and —

C: And I heard Chris telling him, "No, this hurt."

T: Okay. So it sounds like that it really fit our hypothesis in dealing with Joe in this situation, was key in regaining access.

C: Yes. They both said that you have given us hope and that's the first time I have ever heard Chris say that, and that is quite to your credit. I don't know if you know how much of an impact that made, and I know she's not one to say much. But, I want to tell you, "Thank you," because you are, you are the first one.

T: Well, I'm glad that was helpful. I really truly think that you've got a great system and the travesty was that when you could not use the system in a way that it has always worked for you. I really don't see how anyone would want to change your system.

Commentary

Note the questions the therapist asked the client and how many different passes were made to encourage further elaboration of both the change itself and the client's ownership of it. Empowering client change requires the therapist to trust in the probability of change, to recognize when it has occurred, and then to unfold and expand the new perspectives or resolutions that have evolved.

Although we have said this in many different ways, we believe it bears repeating: It is important to trust clients and their inherent abilities to resolve problems. Trusting in the probability of change, both initially and during all phases of treatment, provides opportunities for change by infusing the entire process with hope (Miller et al., 1997). Hope was a key factor with Natalie.

Recognizing change requires a child-like expectation of an inevitable change each time the client returns. In addition to using therapy-generated ideas as opportunities for change, clients often make use of events occurring outside of therapy to resolve their difficulties.

Once Natalie reported that access had been regained, then the focus became a dialogue to expand and further amplify the new perceptions and actions. Further change is empowered through the client's own positive ascriptions without the therapist taking responsibility or assuming a cheerleader role. Natalie seemed to gain momentum for change by describing the changes in the relationship.

Since the client's goal had been met, the therapist now turned to what was next, not making any assumptions about termination or continuation in treatment.

Excerpt Three

T: Now that you have regained access, achieved your goal for seeing me, where do you want to go from here?

C: One of the things that across the board we had wanted to ask you about was how can we help ourselves in our reaction to the Epstein-Barr?

T: Um, okay.

C: It has been debilitating for us. We've lost a very good job. We have had to turn down commissions for murals. We were invited to an international mural conference as guest of honor and we could not go because of this. People just don't get asked to do that every day.

T: Umhm.

C: And I find, I know I am exceedingly angry. The others are just real depressed.

T: Okay.

C: And Chris said she's just going to rely on my anger to keep us moving. She has a point. It is.

T: Umhm.

C: Even in the job we're doing now, we have had to reduce to a four-day work week and we are always in bed.

T: That is depressing.

C: And we're sick of this.

T: Umhm.

C: So I do want to ask for help in how we can help ourselves. I'm sure that there is some grieving that has to go on, and as far as I'm concerned, we're comparing us to the late great us.

T: Umhm. You're grieving the way things used to be for you versus the way you are now. You're constantly comparing.

C: Yes, yeah. We're in that stupid bed asleep and we live with pain. We are in physical pain. We're one of the lucky ones who also, as a result of the Epstein-Barr, we have fibromyalgia. And we live in pain all the time.

T: That is depressing. What are you doing to help your Epstein-Barr?

C: For six weeks we have been getting a B12 shot. They have boosted our vitamin intake. In addition to the multivitamin, we are taking increased beta carotene, increased E, increased C, and a B supplement complex on top.

T: Okay.

C: And we're still dragging and we're still hurting and we're still crawling in bed. And sometime you just don't want to because you're sick of being in the damn bed. And we have significantly adjusted our diet.

T: Okay. So you've done all of the things that they suggested.

C: Yeah, we've been trying.

T: And that's not having any large impact on your health.

C: No. All the books I've read on Epstein-Barr say there's fifteen percent that are debilitated for the rest of their lives. Well, I don't want to be one of those.

T: Boy, that is depressing, it's the loss of your major way of being. You recognize it every time you get out of bed. You recognize that you don't feel like you used to feel.

C: Yes. I went to the library. I have dug everything up I could find and read. I have written to the National Chronic Fatigue Syndrome Association, figuring any information I could get has got to be helpful somehow.

T: Umhm. Well you really sought out information to try to help yourself, but there's never been information that helped all that much.

C: We're doing everything that there is. So we would really appreciate any suggestions you might have to deal with Epstein-Barr.

T: I need to give that some thought. It sounds like you are doing everything humanly possible.

C: Yes. It has affected us across the board.

T: Okay. Who has the least amount of fatigue?

C: Me.

T: Okay. Do you know why it's different for you or how you are able to deal with it better?

C: No, all I know is that it is easier and that's the reason I'm out.

T: Well, it's nice to meet you. I certainly haven't had any trouble liking the three of you that I've seen. You are all very likable.

C: Well, thank you. Thank you very much. And thank you again for believing that being multiple does not make you bad. We've had so many people tell us we were dysfunctional and no we weren't. I mean you don't achieve some of the things we achieved by being dysfunctional.

T: That's for sure.

C: So that just to me is a crock. And I'm angry at having been told we have to merge and aiming therapy in that way. No we don't! We don't want to lose the little ones.

T: That was a bad situation. I will put my mind to work on the Epstein-Barr and give that some thought. I meet regularly with a group of therapists and I'll throw that out for the group to think about.

Commentary

Natalie, actually Gretchen, identified another problem to work on in therapy. She wanted to address ways of dealing with the Epstein-Barr virus. As with the accessing problem, the therapist followed the client's lead regarding the topics discussed. The therapist explored for solution attempts, looking for possibilities. It was obvious that Natalie was trying lots of different avenues to help herself. It was also apparent that she knew far more about it than her therapist. Once again, the therapist validated the client and the client responded with her anger at previous treatments, as well as her appreciation for the therapist's belief in her (them).

As discussed under "taking your own pulse," the therapist mentioned consulting with colleagues. He was quite pleased with the progress so far, but did not want to offer any hasty suggestions. This was his acknowledgment to himself to go slowly and reflect carefully about this rapidly moving and somewhat exotic case.

The therapist met with colleagues and ideas were shared revolving around relaxation and visualization. It was thought that imagery could build upon the client's already intact visualization skills. His colleagues were supportive and encouraged him to continue to do what was working best: listening and relying on the client to provide direction. The team meeting left the therapist feeling prepared for the next session, but nothing could have prepared the therapist for the next session.

SESSION FIVE

Excerpt One

C: This is bizarre. I am Nora and I haven't been out in seven years. And I am trying to figure out why I am here now.

T: Okay. Well . . . [long pause of total befuddlement]. What I can tell you is that Natalie started seeing me because you weren't able to access your alters, and that was very distressing. And that was primarily related to the situation with the man she lives with, Joe. And being the very capable and resourceful person, and people, that she is, she overcame that rather quickly. She then identified another problem that she wanted to work on, the Epstein-Barr. So that was what I was expecting to deal with today. And you apparently haven't been out since 1986?

C: No.

T: So you find yourself in a completely different world. And you've not been aware of anything that has been happening since then. That's mind boggling, to put it mildly.

C: Yeah, I relate to that. I'm wondering what has happened and why I am here now. Why I am needed? Because obviously I have something the others do not.

T: Okay. I think that's an excellent point because the system has been so coherent—the person needed the most tends to come out. And the first thing that has come to my mind was can you, somehow, more effectively deal with the Epstein-Barr? Is that the reason you're out?

C: What is it?

T: I don't understand it all that well, but it's a medical condition caused by a virus that is very debilitating. The person feels very tired, and gets sick easily and has various body aches and pains, and there's really no treatment for it except taking very good care of yourself, eating right, sleeping right, and relaxing.

C: You just gave me a very important clue. Are you familiar with Tai Chi and Akido?

T: Just on a very surface level.

C: I am very well versed in both. Part of the training is spirit with the heart in harmony with the body. I am quite capable of centering. So obviously the system is still functioning.

T: Great! You find yourself out now, when your particular resources and skills are most needed, which certainly fits the way the system works. It is a delightful system.

C: So where do we go from here? I suspect that's probably why I'm here.

T: Perhaps we could explore ways you could help everyone else with the Epstein-Barr. Because that was our intention today, and you're here to deal with that because you're the best one to deal with it.

Commentary

In all the different clinical situations the therapist has observed and participated, never had he felt so initially overwhelmed and confused, and then had such crystal clarity to emerge from the conversation. He did not have to worry about TC or attribution creep because he was so astonished by the client's announcement that all he could do was listen.

Nora had not been "out" for seven years, but recognized that there had to be a reason for her appearance. She was initially concerned about attending the session (which had been journaled for efficient communication), but was reassured by what she read about the therapist.

Excerpt Two

C: And Joe kept calling me Chris but I didn't have time to contradict him, which is okay.

T: Umhm.

C: I'd just as soon he didn't even know I was out for awhile, because at this point right now I don't know what I feel. I'm still in shock finding out it's 1993 and that I'm not in New York.

T: Umhm. That's enough right there.

C: I'm just kinda in shock. I would have liked [slight laugh] to have known who the guy was I was sleeping with! My last memory is that I was at the home of my sensei. . . . I think I am going to have to do some reading, because other than what you told me, I really do not know about Epstein-Barr.

T: There's a lot of information that everyone else has and I guess especially Chris, Gretchen, and Nat are all quite knowledgeable about Epstein-Barr . . . Gretchen asked about other possibilities and one of the things I had discussed with my colleagues was the use of imagery because there's such a wonderful visualization skill that's shared in terms of the way that personalities are accessed. The way Nat described it was like rooms and a separate house.

C: Umhm.

T: And that there's a path—

C: Yes, yes.

T: That you follow and reach—

C: There are.

T: And go to a room and there would be the different alters.

C: Yes, that's how I've always found everyone.

T: So obviously this visualization or imagery has been a pretty important part to the system, and so why not utilize that shared strength as a way to combat the Epstein-Barr?

C: Okay. Sounds good. Why don't we address it?

T: Okay. What I was going to do is talk about ways to use the visualization to combat the Epstein-Barr. These techniques are based on research that has been done with cancer patients where if they were taught to visualize the cells fighting the cancer, that sometimes, the cancer could be—

C: Put into remission.

T: Yes, put into remission, exactly.

C: Okay.

T: You start it with relaxation exercises and then add a visualization component in which your body's resources are rallied to fight the Epstein-Barr, overcome it, and win. You would have to fine-tune a vision that came totally from your experience.

C: What it sounds like is it's not that much different than centering. Well, I don't know if I have the words but I think maybe I can show you. You, you gather yourself. I don't even have to go through the deep breathing ritual any more. If you're beginning it helps. You gather yourself [demonstrates] and then you feel the energy here [points to chest]. And then from that energy, you push it or you sustain it. But you gather yourself and then once you are centered, your mind can think. You'll find you're in a different state. And even that little bit I have lost some tenseness.

T: Okay, great! I'm completely convinced that that's why you're here. You are here to marshal your energies to overcome or alleviate the effects of the Epstein-Barr. You are the one the system believed could best do it.

C: I agree. Akido is a way of fighting, but it is a defensive fighting. It is not offensive.

T: Umhm, umhm, and the only thing that I know about Akido is that its art is defensive and you also utilize the energy of your opponent.

C: Yes, you can draw it to you. And you can turn it against them.

T: Umhm. And perhaps that's the metaphor for what you need to do with Epstein-Barr. It's been increasingly more distressing for all of you that you've not been able to do some of the things that you've been wanting to do. You've been giving up conferences.

C: I think you would have made a good sensei. That's a compliment. You seem to try to look into the heart and apply some logical thought with compassion.

T: Thank you. Since you already know how to do centering and marshaling energy, you can begin to think about how you can apply that as you learn more about Epstein-Barr. Probably, as you learn about that, you will receive some kind of confirmation about that's why you're here, would be my guess.

C: Okay.

T: The only thing that I didn't mention to you was that Nat told me that you all have always hoped for co-consciousness, which would certainly make life easier.

C: Really, that would be great.

Commentary

Discussion revealed that Nora had a black belt in marshal arts and was quite adept at centering, focusing, and self-discipline—exactly the skills required to rally her resources to overcome Epstein-Barr. The elegance of the system was apparent once again. The therapist stayed within the client's frame of reference, trusting in the wisdom of her system. Nora's task was to educate herself about Epstein-Barr and think of ways to visualize its defeat.

SESSION SIX

Excerpt One

T: So, how are you today?

C: I would say substantially better than the last time you saw me [laughs].

T: Okay. So you're Nora.

C: Yes. I've been doing a lot of catch-up. One thing I am sure of, I am here to deal with the Epstein-Barr. The Epstein-Barr is something that eats away at your immune system from inside. We have been doing everything medically that can be done.

T: Umhm.

C: And it's still a downward spiral.

T: Uh-huh.

C: So that's why I've been drug out of the closet.

T: Okay.

C: I was out after our car accident when we were getting patterned for crawling and walking again. I was able to make it stick.

T: Okay. So you were drug out of the closet for that medical crisis as well. Boy, that would make complete sense that you would find your way back out now.

C: I have been thinking a lot about applying my skills to the Epstein-Barr. Let me give an example. One time I cut myself pretty significantly. And it was throbbing, but I had to get something done before I could take care of it.

T: Umhm.

C: So I went to the thumb and I quote "closed it."

T: Exactly! That's exactly it.

C: Okedoke, because I did. I quote "closed it" and then it let me finish what I had to do.

T: That's wonderful. Well that's why you're out [laughs]. That's why you're here.

C: Okay, so that's what you're referring to. Okay, and then when I am able to successfully do that, somehow translate and send that across to the others.

T: Yes. They would need to learn the skills. You already have all the skills because you know how to focus and relax, and you are able to take control of a physical phenomenon.

C: Yes, yes.

T: So you can already do that so you have all the skills necessary. But it would be great if you teach the others —

C: Get it across to the others.

Commentary

Nora researched Epstein-Barr and unequivocally confirmed that she was out to address the illness. She noted how she had previously been "drug out of the closet" to deal with a medical crisis. More importantly, she had already been successful at what she needed to do with the Epstein-Barr: She had taken control of a cut and stopped the bleeding.

The therapist accepted the client at face value and followed her lead because it was apparent she knew precisely where to go and what to do. The rest of the session was spent discussing the metaphor that Nora would use to combat the Epstein-Barr. Although in retrospect it became very significant, at the time the therapist didn't pay much attention to the client's comments about getting the skills across to the other alters. Had he noticed, he might have had some indication to where Nora's efforts might lead.

SESSION SEVEN

Excerpt One

T: Well, so how are you doing?

C: Well, I'm ah, good, different. I wanted to ask you if you wanted a hug but I didn't know if it would be proper or not. Ahm, I'm integrated.

T: You're integrated [very overwhelmed]!

C: Or, I don't know if I raised the right word but everybody's there.

T: Wow, that's pretty incredible.

C: It happened last Friday night and I'm a me and I'm a different me. That's why I asked you if you wanted a hug but didn't know if that would be appropriate or not.

T: That would be fine. That's incredible! How did that happen?

C: When Nora was working on visualization for Epstein-Barr, she said it ought to be able to be applied to the barriers between us, and she told everybody to try to imagine themselves all in the library at the same time visiting. And Nat was out and she called a friend, Sonya, the two have been very close, and she has been a good friend to us as a whole too. She accepted everybody. And Nat knew something was going to happen. She didn't know what, but she needed someone there who could help her through it. And also, while we do not attend church, we're pretty devout and Sonya is too, and I know it's going to sound pretty bizarre, but Sonya had just the right scripture and they prayed and Sonya said everybody came forth. She said that one person after another came out, and everybody had gifts to bring, and said "I belong."

T: That's wonderful.

C: And [pause] I'm, I'm a me and I'm different.

T: This is a really remarkable turn of events, and I'm kind of overwhelmed by it. Actually, I'm a little surprised that you're pleased with it.

C: Everybody's there. And if they want they could still come out, but I'm a me.

T: Okay. Okay. So everybody is all there. No one had to go away or be absorbed—

C: No.

T: Rather, everyone is still there for you to access but yet it's integrated because—

C: I'm a me.

T: Well that's wonderful!

C: And I am artistic. I have had, that happened Friday, there have been eight days of no pain, no body pain either.

T: Well that's wonderful. You mean no pain, no body pain from the Epstein-Barr?

C: No.

T: That's great! Well, that's wonderful news. That's super. I'm really glad to hear that.

C: Me too. We had been eating Advil around the clock just because the pain was to where it was intolerable.

T: Umhm.

C: It's been eight days.

T: That's wonderful. So you have maintained this me-ness [laughs] since last Friday and you're attributing it to Nora working on the Epstein-Barr and she figured out a way to essentially break down the barriers between all of you, and bring you all together, but still retaining the distinctiveness of all of the people.

C: Yes. It's still like I can hear voices [laughs]. And I know that sounds really crazy. [Both laugh]

T: Yeah, you don't want to broadcast that to too many people. But that is essentially what, co-consciousness? Would you call it that?

C: I think so. But, I am a me and this me is finding things out [laughs]. I'm finding a lot of things out. I'm articulate. I have movement. I definitely have a temper [laughs], and I can express it [laughs]. I have a very warped sense of humor. I'm finding a lot of things out. It's like I'm looking through a pair of new eyes that have never been touched or scarred. I don't know if that makes sense but that's what it feels like.

T: It makes complete sense. It sounds like a rebirthing.

C: And I'm a me [laughs]. Those were the first words out of my mouth, I'm a me.

T: That's great. That's wonderful.

C: It's amazing, and I'm grateful on one hand, but I expected the other shoe to drop and things just to go kaput and it hasn't, and there have been some stressful things with Joe [laughs]. And then I got angry and I didn't take any shit back.

T: That's fantastic. Sounds like you are handling Joe. That's terrific. It's been like a whole new world to you.

C: It is. I mean it really is. I'm sculpting and I'm sketching my own ideas. I'm just amazed [beaming with pride].

T: And now you feel like you have the energy to tackle it. You look real energetic.

C: I almost even bounce when I walk [both laugh]. I don't know if this is just a high, but it's lasted eight days so I think maybe I am kind of bubbly anyway. And I wake up bubbly.

T: That's great. It's amazing. And Nora coming out seems to be the kick-off point—

C: Yes.

T: And your read of it is that she somehow applied her abilities to break down the barriers, that gathered everyone into the library, and that from there your friend came over and prayed and read scripture.

C: Yeah. And then it was like everyone started coming forward. Sonya said it started with Teresa and it was quite obvious that it was a three-year-old with a speech defect, and she brought giggles, and she said she belonged and she liked peanut butter and jelly sandwiches. Sonya said my face was changing the whole time.

T: Uh-huh. Quite a turn of events. It sounds like you have achieved the co-consciousness that you wanted. You were able to integrate without giving everybody up or losing anybody.

C: And that was crucial. That just could not be. That was not acceptable.

T: And you have figured out a way to do it without giving anybody up. Everyone is still there. That's great. Yeah, integrated, but without casting aside anyone.

C: Yeah, and [laughs] I'm a brand new something.

T: Just like you had your own system, quite unique, very healthy and functional, now you've figured out your own way of integrating and having co-consciousness. People who think of integration tend to think of melding with the others being gone.

C: Right, and instead I think what everybody did was created a me. We did it backwards or inside out. Every body is there and the reading that I had done is that quite a few of them went away. It was like they were discarded and that's not right. That's just not right. Instead, I'm a me—everyone came together and said let's share. That's what happened.

T: Umhm. Okay. So that's different. Everybody came to share qualities and characteristics and parts of themselves to create you. So you're a creation of the system's sharing.

C: Yes. Because I have Gretchen's movement. I have Nat's intuition because I can tell you are feeling pretty good about all this, I've got Chris's organization because I've already prioritized things in terms of what's important. I am articulate and have a command of French. I also speak Spanish. I have a slight command of Japanese.

T: That's great. That's wonderful.

C: That's why I am sure it is a sharing.

T: That's wonderful! That's fantastic. The whole thing is starting to come together for me. It makes so much sense to me now. The image of bringing everybody together in the library, and rather than them crumbling into nothingness and then you emerging, it's more like they collaboratively shared parts of themselves to come up with you. Well you're the best of all worlds. You are a collection of their best assets.

C: Of their values, what they call their gifts.

T: Their gifts. Okay, that's beautiful. The metaphor is now sinking into my head!

C: [Laughs] It's their gifts! That's why there is no hardness here. And there is a peacefulness. And I haven't been scarred.

T: Right, that's not a part of the gifts you have been given.

C: No, and it means I have a chance of dealing with the world fresh. It means I can treat my dad with compassion. I can treat mom with compassion.

T: That's really remarkable.

C: I think that is a wonderful gift.

T: That's a great gift. Pretty amazing, pretty amazing. Great, great, your own unique way of doing it.

C: Figures [laughs].

T: Really! It definitely figures. You had your own unique way of being multiple, your own unique coherent system, you own way of operating and . . . you couldn't let go of your alters.

C: It would have been a death.

T: Umhm, a death.

C: And that sucked. It wasn't and it's not acceptable. I mean there was another answer. And I'm wondering if our answer could be shared by some other multiples and maybe helped.

T: Umhm. It could be very helpful to a lot of multiples who are not given the opportunity to think of themselves as having gifts to share rather than having identities to break down.

C: Yeah, they have gifts to share, and everybody brought gifts. *I think I am a collage of those gifts.* A walking, living, breathing collage of those gifts.

T: Umhm, and what more could a person ask for? To be the shared gifts of so many people who are gifted.

C: I think they're all pretty wonderful.

T: Umhm, umhm. You have really literally pulled together here. [Both laugh]

C: Yes. This is a major monument.

T: Oh yeah, this is what you have been striving for your whole life.

C: Yes.

T: The first times I saw Nat she said, "We'd really love to have co-consciousness. We would like to have everyone still here but have some kind of integration of all of us." And you've gotten that.

C: That is what they've done and I'm a me and here I am.

T: You were a superstar before in a lot of ways. The only thing holding you back was the Epstein-Barr and the Joe situation. You've worked through that and you're ready to go like a rocket-ship now.

C: Yeah. Thank you.

T: You're welcome. Thank you! You know you really made my day. I'm really glad to hear all this. You are a remarkable person.

C: Thanks.

T: It is a great celebration!

C: Yes it is. Yes it is. Wow. Well, thanks a lot.

T: You feel like a hug?

C: Yeah. [The therapist and Natalie hug]

DISCUSSION

If we had any doubts before, this case convinced us of the idiosyncratic strengths and resources of human beings and the inherent beauty found in human diversity. Natalie announced that she had become whole. She said, "I am a me." The therapist was overwhelmed, awestruck, and genuinely speechless. Reiterating, never had a case impacted the therapist in such a profound way. In a very eloquent way, Natalie shared her experience of integrating without losing anyone.

It was Nora who had been the catalyst for the change. Nora, while working on the Epstein-Barr problem, figured out how to break down the barriers between the alters. Through visualization, Nora had gathered all the alters. Each alter brought a gift to contribute. These collective gifts emerged into an integrated whole. Natalie, therefore, was representative of the best of what each alter had to offer; she was a collage of those gifts! Her system was still intact and she knew that everyone was okay. She visualized them sitting comfortably in the library, chatting and watching her.

The therapist could never have predicted such an outcome. In the span of seven sessions, this incredibly talented woman had rallied her resources and integrated her personalities in a way that was acceptable to her. She did it *her* way. This occurred without intervention regarding integration by the therapist and without reliance on any theory of treatment or integration of multiples. Instead, the therapist relied on and believed in the client, accommodated her frame of reference, and honored her theory of change. Left to her own devices, she implemented her unique method of integration, and accomplished her own personal co-consciousness.

This case helped us to appreciate the power of our clients—their abilities to overcome adversity and make satisfactory lives for themselves. The therapist saw Natalie in three follow-up sessions and two couple sessions with Joe, spanning 15 months; she has maintained her sense of "me."

CHAPTER 7

Case Example: Delusional Disorder
or "Surviving Until Retirement"

While we pursue the unattainable we make impossible the realizable.

Robert Ardrey

WE NOW PRESENT THE impossible case of Alice, a woman diagnosed with a delusional (paranoid) disorder. This chapter follows the format of discussing the existing views of treatment, identifying the pathways to impossibility, and presenting session dialogue, accompanied by commentary detailing our clinical style and methods. After an abbreviated review of recent thinking regarding delusional disorder and its management, Alice and her husband, David, are introduced.

This chapter demonstrates how a person considered psychotic by her husband, doctor, and previous mental health provider finds a way out of her dilemma and saves face.

DELUSIONAL DISORDER:
TREATMENT RECOMMENDATIONS

Overview

Delusional (paranoid) disorder is of unknown etiology. It comprises a diverse group of disorders, the hallmark or identifying feature being the formation and persistence of a delusion. Afflicted individuals exhibit nonbizarre delusions, patently false beliefs that could actually occur in real life (e.g., being followed, a victim of a loved one's infidelity, or malevolently treated). The delusional disorders, moreover, are thought to be distinct from schizophrenia, mood disorders, and organically-sponsored conditions, such as drug-induced toxic states and infectious or metabolic diseases. Unlike the kind of personality deterioration observed in the schizophrenias, the delusional client comes across as unimpaired in functioning. In addition, the emotional and behavioral responses to the delusion appear appropriate (Manschreck, 1989).

Delusional disorder with delusions of infidelity, the label applied in the case to be discussed, has also been called the Othello syndrome, amorous paranoia, conjugal paranoia, or pathologic jealousy. It is usually described in males with no history of psychiatric disorder. Manschreck (1989) notes that the delusion of infidelity may appear suddenly and come to explain a "host of present and past events involving the spouse's infidelity" (p. 825). This disorder is believed to be difficult to treat, relinquished only on the occurrence of marital separation, divorce, or the death of the spouse.

Nash (1983) suggests that the disorder arises in feelings of inadequacy and diminished self-esteem, compounded by ambivalence and hatred. During the "illness," casual events are misinterpreted and then submitted to intense focus. The object of the jealousy is then subjected to accusations, leading sometimes to self-fulfilling prophecies. In time, the client becomes certain, through the action of projective mechanisms, that the loved one is unfaithful (Nash).

Although delusions represent a most dramatic dilemma, delusional disorders are believed to be uncommon. Systematic, large-scale studies of this complaint are equally rare and the field's knowledge base rests principally on case studies. What data are available indicate the disorder generally does not lead to severe impairment. A favorable prognosis has been associated with a more acute and earlier onset, the presence of precipitating factors, and being both female and married (Manschreck, 1989).

Treatment

As delusional disorders are psychotic by definition, antipsychotic medication has been used. Owing to the rarity of the condition and the paucity of controlled studies, the kinds of results necessary to support the practice are few and uncertain. Antipsychotic drugs are said to work best with clients "whose psychotic symptoms are florid, acute and accompanied by anxiety and agitation" (Frances, Clarkin, & Perry, 1984, p. 191; Manschreck, 1989; Walker & Cavenar, Jr., 1983).

On the basis of current knowledge, no school of psychotherapy can claim any special expertise in the treatment of paranoid disorders. Psychotherapeutic approaches rest principally on supportive measures. The therapist should avoid arguments with the client and should not attempt to placate by appearing to agree with the delusion (Kaplan, Sadock, & Grebb, 1994; Nash, 1983; Shea, 1988). It is also recommended that the client should be informed "of the presence of a mental disorder leading to disturbed thinking" (Nash, 1983, p. 478) while allowing the client to report the delusions without the therapist's judgment.

A notable exception to this convention of treatment is provided by Fraser (1983). Coming out of an Ericksonian and MRI strategic tradition of symptom utilization, Fraser suggested that treatment should involve accepting the delusions and suggesting different, more constructive behaviors based on the delusions.

Anything constituting a standard of care for delusional disorder is hard, if not impossible to find. As with many clinical problems, opinion and conjecture have the upper hand over empirically established treatment protocols. It is generally agreed that an insight-oriented approach is to be avoided for supportive therapy. Owing to the intense feelings of these clients and their insistence on the veracity of a false belief, considerable patience and skill is counseled.

THE CASE OF ALICE

For eighteen months, Alice, a 65-year-old homemaker, has become increasingly distressed. She steadfastly believes that David, her husband, is having an affair. David vehemently denies Alice's accusations and, along with their family doctor and previous counselor, wants her medicated. Alice often stays up all night, crying and pacing the floor. She scrutinizes David's every behavior and frequently follows him to work.

When making the appointment, Alice told the therapist about her husband being involved with a neighbor at their vacation home, and about her belief that David was keeping another woman, either from the bank or their dentist's office.

SESSION ONE

Excerpt One

A: Well, where do I start today?
T: From our phone conversation, when you made the appointment to see me, it's obvious that you have a very strong belief that David is fooling around.
A: I just want for him to stop.
T: And that would be your major goal for coming here, for him to stop fooling around.
A: Right. That's exactly what I'm here for.

Commentary

Mindful of the importance of establishing an alliance with the client as a bridge to her participation, the therapist takes this opportunity very early in the session to reach agreement on goals. He then invites Alice to elaborate her vision of what will be happening when the goal is reached.

Excerpt Two

T: How will you know when he stops?
A: I think that the way he does things would change. The things that he does just tip you off. Like, before he gets ready to go to work some days, he can't sit still, he's red in the face, he rubs his face, he rubs his eyes. He gets up sometimes and brushes his teeth twice before he goes to work. It's just the things he does makes me know that he is up to something. On days he isn't, he's not that way, you know.
T: Uh-huh.
A: And [sighs] well you live with him 45 years and if he does anything different, it's just, you just know, you know. OH! [Big sigh and starts crying] Sometimes I just get up and get in the car and

leave, because I can't watch him anymore. If it wasn't for my car, I don't know what I'd do. And I've tried everything, you know, I've told him everything. . . . I've tried everything, talked to him to try to get him to stop and nothing works. I think it's hopeless. I thinks it's just went so far, it's hopeless. I really think maybe he can't help it anymore.

T: Sounds like it's pretty awful for you.

A: Oh, it is, just terrible. Now, my dad was this way. Oh, my mother went through hell with him. And, I went through that trying to stick with her. But he accused mom of running around with other men, and here mom's just a little religious thing, never done nothing to nobody. And, now David never accuses me of that because he knows better, he knows that I think too much of my marriage, I wouldn't do that for nothing. The worst part is he's laying it all off on me, saying that I'm sick and need help. Tells that to the doctor, and this other counselor the doctor sent us to. And they believed him! Doctor said I was suffering from paranoid, and talked me into taking medicine. I took it for three weeks is all. But then no way. I'm never going back to that doctor. Counselor was the same thing. I'm not sick, and I sure ain't crazy. David is so slick. You know what I'm saying? But, this is the only way that he can accept what he's doing. He's got to blame it on somebody else, because this man is—all his life had so much morals, okay? I mean, he was a stickler for morals and everything, so this is a complete turnaround for him.

T: Right out of character. Doesn't sound like your concerns got addressed in the other counseling.

Commentary

In a very short time, Alice moves from a statement of her goal to sharing the depth of her pain. She greatly fears a repetition of her mother's experience—one that apparently made an indelible print on her life. She also shares her frustration and dissatisfaction with former treaters.

The therapist listens and accommodates his comments to help Alice experience him as interested in and concerned with her point of view. This step in the building of the alliance is crucial as the client makes it clear that she had no alliance with her former treaters. To them, she was sick. She is not about to accept this label from anyone.

Excerpt Three

A: I went along for a while, thinking they would try and see my side of things, but they didn't. Counselor kept trying to tell me David was a good husband and just trying to go to work. Kept trying to push David's story on me. He can't live with it, you know, really. And it's tearing him up. I told him, I said, "One of us is going to have a heart attack or stroke over this." I said, "Here we are ready to retire," which the first of April it's supposed to start, and I said, "The best time of our life and we are in this shape?" [Really crying now] It's just terrible!

T: Sad, very sad.

A: But there's just times that I just look at him and I can't handle no more of it. I don't know if there is any answer, you know? It's just went so far, I don't think there is an answer. And this business about money coming out of his check every week. He's either keeping somebody—he's obsessed with that too. Sometimes I feel like throwing in the towel and forget the whole thing. But, I care too much about my marriage for that.

T: You have a lot invested in it.

A: It's just I still love him [crying]. I've tried everything, I don't know what to do. There's just times I can't hardly handle it. And it doesn't seem to stop no matter what you say to him. I say, I try and tell him that, "Here you have two little grandsons. You're the only grandfather they've got." I said, "If you and me split up, the kids aren't going to have nothing to do with you. Your family—you'd be lost without your family. You're a family man. You think all you need is a younger woman. What if that don't work out? There's many people at our age that have this kind of trouble that split up. And that don't work and you just made a mess of your lives."

T: That's true.

A: And I try and point this stuff out to him but the way he is right now, I don't think it sinks in. And, I don't deserve this because I haven't done anything to him. He's the one who's stepped over the line. It wasn't me. And so I just don't think it's fair. He doesn't worry about me, he knows I'm at home. He's perfectly satisfied with that as long as I don't interfere in what he's doing. Oh, he'll hug on you and kiss you and stuff. If he gets smoochy before he goes to work, forget it. You're in trouble that day because he's up to something. I really think that he helped this woman buy a car. And I think he's either given her the money to pay on that or he's paying all the time, I don't know which. Because everything points to it. And if he's this serious about this woman and he's bought her a car, can you see him giving her up? I can't!

T: That's a lot of money to invest in a person.

A: I don't know where it's all going to end. Here we both worked our you-know-whats off to get where we are at now. Ohhh! This is pitiful. He don't know what he's doing. And I hate that too because this man always had so much morals and everything. I never even questioned, never! I never seen his check or anything until this started. But then when he took out that secret savings account and I accidentally found out about that, I was really hurt. So, that really hurt me. He swears he ain't doing it, but I know just exactly what he pays. I know where all of his money goes and I know how much he has left. So it isn't hard to figure. He's paying on this woman's car. And it's usually missing on Friday night when he comes home from work. So I check his billfold — I never did that before either. First time I did that I felt like a louse [starts to cry]. You know, it stinks.

T: It does.

A: Something just happened, I don't know what. Same thing happened to dad. Lord, it did give mama ulcers and everything else, she just . . . it was just so pitiful. But he used to come home in the middle of the night and then, the same thing David does, and then [snaps fingers] it was over and he hadn't done nothing. That's the way with David. He puts it out of his mind. He can't live with what he's doing, so therefore, he denies. He puts it in denial, he denies that you've even had a fuss, he denies that he has done anything. It don't matter if you show him the clothes down in the basement with paint all over them. It don't matter if you show him coveralls that you just washed and there is grease all over them. And yet, he hasn't worked on your vehicles. He denies it, the whole thing. So I don't know what to do. I was hoping this would help.

T: Uh-huh.

A: I think he needs medical help. Somebody said it was like a hormone imbalance that happens. I don't know, they just snap all at once. So I'm nervous about the whole thing.

T: No wonder, I don't blame you. Here you have put 45 years into this marriage, been a faithful wife to a good husband, and now right before you retire you find out about this secret savings account and begin noticing other strange things which make you suspicious that he is fooling around. . . . You know, in some ways you are playing a poker game here and you are showing your hand everyday by bringing this up and asking questions and pointing these things out to him, which he always denies, he never admits it. You are kind of showing your hand all the time. And sometimes the only way is—

A: Is to quit showing my hand.

T: Exactly, is to quit showing your hand and then you will find out and have the kind of evidence that will prove it for sure, and you will not have to accept the denial anymore. What I was thinking was that you give some thought to stop bringing it up, stop talking to him about it, but instead, from a distance, observe and make notes on the things that you notice are different. Back off a little bit and let him be lulled into a sense of complacency about it.

A: Uh-huh, you're right because the thing of it is, if I get close to something, just like I found out about the woman down at the bank that he took books to so he could get around her, then he quits that. He stops just short of really being exposed because I let him know I'm smelling a rat. This whole thing is just about more than I can bear.

Commentary

The therapist continues to validate the client's experience. Though it might be tempting to question her explanation of her husband's behavior, he steadfastly avoids doing so. At this point, whether she is "delusional" or merely wrong is irrelevant. Other helpers tried to question or talk her out of her frame of reference and it failed to help. To attempt to do so again would be an enactment of "more of the same," a pathway to impossibility already followed in this case. Instead, the therapist commiserates with Alice, continuing to offer himself as someone who will listen to her and entertain her world view as a legitimate interpretation.

The therapist also floats a possibility for new action for the client to consider. Using the metaphor of gambling, he suggests that by showing her hand (i.e., energetically pursuing him with evidence of his infidelity) she might be playing into her husband's. In short, he accepts her stance as tenable and then proposes different steps for her to follow: back off, observe, and keep her observations to herself. In this way, her husband, no longer vigilant to Alice's fact-finding, might then show his hand.

Most importantly, the therapist's suggestion of a possible way of approaching her concerns explicitly validates her frame of reference regarding David's behavior. Alice accepts this possibility. Whether she immediately acts upon it is less important than for her to consider another way of addressing this conflict with her husband. Indeed, as much as her former treaters were following "more of the same," so too has she succumbed to its power by persisting in a problem-solving strategy that is not working.

Alice's acknowledgment of another way of acting bespeaks flexibility and openness. We attribute this development to Alice's inherent strengths and the therapist's willingness to treat Alice with respect and as a credible person. Alice then proposes her own possibility for new action.

Excerpt Four

T: How are you managing to cope with all this?

A: Listen, you know what I had a notion to do one day? But then I didn't know if that was the thing to do. I thought of sending myself flowers. And send myself flowers and put "from a secret admirer." I was going to get dressed up some night and leave about 10 minutes before he got home from work and then come back in about an hour later. Cause he knows I'm there and he don't have to worry about me.

T: I think you're on the right track with that. I'd like to see you do some of those things. Anything that will help you deal with this mess, because he isn't giving you any satisfaction. The tables will be turned a little bit. Because instead of questioning him, he might start questioning you.

A: Well, that's exactly right. He's like a sly fox, is what he is you know.

T: You got to get slyer, you got to get slyer than him.

Commentary

By the end of the first meeting, the client and therapist are proposing and discussing new and different options for managing her dilemma. This is the language of collaboration, of an alliance in process. To reach this phase, the therapist showed acceptance, compassion, and a readiness to treat the client as a reliable informant on her problem. In short, the therapist honors the client's theory of change.

This was a welcome and novel experience for Alice. Based on her report, her concerns had been diminished and minimized. Regardless of a person's level of ego organization or ultimate diagnostic status, no one likes to feel they are not being taken seriously. Once she feels heard, Alice begins to show not only a receptiveness to altering her behavior, but also creativity. She says she might send flowers to herself, dress up, and break the unhelpful routine she had established with her husband.

Again, at this place in the therapy, what the client finally decides to do is less important that her demonstration of amenability. She may not change her belief about her husband, but she is showing an interest in doing something different with her beliefs. This is a good prognostic sign and one that the therapist will continue to monitor and nurture.

We resume the case with the second session; the therapist meets first with David.

SESSION TWO

Excerpt One

T: How is it going?

D: Ain't been worth a nickel. When we left here Friday, she

wouldn't talk, went to a restaurant, had breakfast, was all upset. Before I got ready to go to work, she gets mad, gets up, heads out the door, and said, "Now you can go call your girlfriend."

T: Okay. She believes you are fooling around with the bank or dentist woman.

D: Yeah!

T: And believes you are paying for her car.

D: Yes. And that's not true; then Saturday and Sunday she was okay. Monday, I come home Monday night, she's been out running the roads, hunting for me or watching for me, seeing if I was seeing anybody. This stuff gets to me! She acted up practically all week. Wednesday she was all upset. I even hate talking about it. What I would really like to see is us get busy, see what we can do for her. Now, I don't know how long this can go on just talking about it. She stays up all night, she didn't sleep. She just acted like a bundle of nerves. Now, I am not lying to you when I tell you this, this is the way she acts. Oh . . . [long drawn-out sigh]. It's not easy talking about it, it really isn't. I mean she acts like, she is just going to have a stroke or a nervous breakdown or something.

T: What made Saturday and Sunday okay?

D: I don't know, you know I don't know, unless she is staying busy.

T: And you are around her those days totally, right? So she knows you are right there with her. She knows then you are not seeing other people.

D: Well, that might be something to it too.

T: So, we need to somehow replicate what happens when you are together all the time. . . . What have you tried to do to respond to her to help?

Commentary

The therapist is getting David's side of the story. As David talks, the therapist hears of an instance of success, a time when the problem is not happening. As solution-focused therapy has taught us, those moments bear investigating. It is at these times a pathway out of impossibility may be found. At the least, the therapist discovers that when Alice and David are together, the problem leaves them alone. He looks for more instances when "more of the same" is put on the run.

David's presentation was dripping with urgency—he wanted something done. He wanted his old wife back. This was certainly understandable given Alice's agitation, distress, and persistent questioning of his behavior. The therapist worked hard to not respond to David's desperation.

Excerpt Two

D: I've tried everything. I am not one to argue. Well I have said I'm not doing this stuff, baby. That's the way I talk to her. I really don't know. I mean, you would have to see her, how she is when she is acting this way. I'm not a very good explainer, I mean, I really have a hard time explaining this stuff because it's whoa— it's hard! I mean, just like she was yesterday. I don't know what to do with her. Isn't there anything you could give her to calm her down?

Commentary

For the moment, Alice's husband deflects the therapist's request to learn more about his efforts to find resolution. He reports his powerlessness and asks the therapist to do something. At this juncture the therapist was struggling with David's sense of urgency, desperation, and desire to have Alice medicated. The therapist found it easier to work within Alice's frame of reference than David's impatience and insistence on quick action. This was a cue for the therapist to take his own pulse. He slowed down, employed a relaxation exercise, listened, and finally resisted the urge to respond to David's desire to calm his wife with medication.

The therapist next agrees he *can* do something to help Alice calm down, pointing out that Alice's participation is key. He gently reminds David of what already has not worked. The therapist is attempting to set the stage for David to take new action to defeat the problem in the marriage. Making Alice the crazy paranoid has not eliminated Alice's seemingly endless accusations.

Excerpt Three

T: Yeah. But you know, she has to want to do that. She has to think that is a good idea too. Or she won't take it. Isn't that what your doctor and the other counselor tried to get her to do, and she then refused to go back to either one of them?

D: Yeah.

T: So, unless she believes that her point of view is taken seriously, she's not going to want to do anything I suggest. If she feels that we are fingering her as the crazy one, I believe we will have a hard time with this.

D: Where does she ever come up with that stuff? I don't know, even picking on this one lady, whew! I don't, I don't know where it came from, to tell you the truth. I think I've bent over backwards in dealing with this thing.

T: Well, you have done a lot already. And you are really sticking with her. I really admire that.

D: I love the woman.

T: I guess what we are trying to do is throw a monkey wrench into this thing, whatever has caused it. And then sometimes a person, without admitting it, will just let it go. If you think it's a good idea, one suggestion would be to stop trying to convince her that you are not having an affair. In other words, not respond to her with defending yourself. Avoiding any accuser-defender business. Instead, when she makes an accusation, what I suggest is that you say back to her, "You are afraid that I am having an affair with another women. I'm not going to try to convince you with my words anymore, Alice, because I know you think I am and you are entitled to your belief." I am suggesting that you not defend yourself, or attempt to convince her of your innocence, because it is not working. You can't convince her because for one, if she admits she's been wrong, she'll be admitting that you and the doctor and counselor were right about her being crazy. I guess I don't think that she will ever do it.

D: That's true. She can't be convinced. She is a stubborn mule!

T: Sometimes when you stop trying to convince someone of something, they figure it out on their own.

Commentary

The therapist benefits from taking his pulse and compliments David for his devotion to his wife, a real strength in the face of trying circumstances. As with Alice, he makes no attempt to get to the real truth about the alleged affairs and accepts what the couple has to say about their predicament. To do to David what Alice has done, will probably not work.

David has made his position quite clear. Accordingly, the therapist is trying to be an honest broker to both Alice and him, implying that the problem, whatever its origin, is the real culprit. It is a "thing" in need of a "monkey wrench."

The therapist also sensitively implies that Alice will require a way to save face. To admit she is wrong is a concession she will not make to anyone who labeled her crazy. In effect, to do so is to agree to a major invalidation. Curiously, after making this observation David refers to his wife as a "stubborn mule." This description, though perhaps removed from loving tribute, is better than his making a psychiatric assessment. If he continues to regard her as stubborn rather than crazy, there will be more possibilities for him to consider. Only professionals, not distraught husbands, can manage mental illness.

Session two continues with the therapist meeting with Alice.

Excerpt Four

T: I'm just worrying about how, when he does straighten up, how he's going to convince you that he has. I don't know how he's ever going to be able to convince you that he's not doing it anymore.

A: I think after he retires. Now see he's fine on the weekends because he's with me, okay?

T: Okay. Can you tell me what else is different about the weekends?

A: I wouldn't let him go any place without me on purpose. I thought, whoever it is, you're just not going to see him this weekend. This is my weekend and you're not going to do it. And I don't like doing that way with him.

Commentary

In this brief excerpt, the therapist suggests that in the future the problem will be over and what will be left is how to cope with the aftermath. Alice also sees an end to the problem once David retires. She confirms that weekends now work for the couple, but concedes that she does not like her watchful possessiveness. She is regarding this aspect of her behavior as "ego-dystonic"—it is not fitting with the way she wants to be with her husband.

With the second session completed, additional progress has been made to defeat an impossible dilemma. Alice and David are aware of moments of liberation from the problem. Both have had their respective positions, their unique frames of reference, accepted and validated. David has made a small, but meaningful shift in describing his wife as stubborn and understands that labeling her as crazy will get him nowhere. Alice envisions a brighter future ahead with her husband's retirement and expresses disappointment with her own behavior. The therapist has proposed new courses of action for the couple to contemplate, which have not been rejected out of hand.

As seen in the next session, the task ahead is to continue to cement the alliance with the couple and explore possibilities as they arise. The therapist consults with colleagues and discusses his difficulties with David's urgent requests for medication. The team suggests that the therapist focus on Alice's desires for therapy, and concentrate on honoring David's understandable anxiety.

SESSION THREE

Excerpt One

A: Also there's another thing I wanted to tell ya that I didn't get around to. Now I went to do the wash, and there's black hairs all over his undershorts. Four pairs of them. I mean not just a few black hairs, okay, I think that tells the tale! And I was furious and 'course I went and told him.

T: He denied it.

A: Right! He won't admit to nothin'. I hope you're keeping an open mind about this because it's too early to form an opinion, but I thought I'd let you know how serious this is. The others formed an opinion too soon.

T: I have an open mind to it. I believe you have good reason for your suspicions. You mean the other counselor and your doctor.

A: Yeah, they believed David, he's awful slick you know. He probably does it at supper time, and they'd get in the car probably. I decided that he had a woman up there at supper time. Yeah, see this is the kind of things he does to me all the time, and it makes me feel this big. Every time I see it I just get upset.

T: So the hairs on the underwear has happened more than one time?

A: And, and if not that you can tell if he's hot, okay? You can tell from his undershorts, you know what I mean, you can tell he's been hot,

T: Okay.

A: Okay? When I seen them hairs on his undershorts, it was awful, and he denies everything, he just denies everything.

T: He just says no —

A: Ain't no way . . . is what his main thing is that he says. You know, he thinks he's got you convinced that he didn't do a thing. I just went along with it. And he just acts superior about the whole thing see? He thinks he's got you where he wants you, okay? Just like the other counselor and our doctor. You believe everything he says . . . But I know you don't.

T: Well, I've got an open mind to it —

A: Like this woman down there — bought that car for her, I still believe it. I found out where she got the car, I talked to the man. Here's a woman whose got two cars, ya know what I'm saying to you? I walked into the place, and I walked right up to the man who sold her the car. So, I asked him, did you have a car sold to so and so in June or July? He said, yep, and I said was there a tall, dark-haired man in his sixties with her? He said, no, and I said where'd she finance it, and he said it was personal financing. They didn't go through no company, no nothing. Okay, everything points. So it's the little things that happen, all you have to do is put two and two together. So what if he pays all this money to her, then what?

T: You're worried that he will leave you for her?

A: Yeah, I'm scared to death. It happened to my mom.

T: That is really tragic, and you fear you may be facing the same fate.

A: Well, I guess deep down I don't think he would do it, but given what he's been doing, who knows!

T: Hmm, but, you had a real good weekend again though.

A: Yeah, oh yeah, he's good as gold to me on the weekends.

T: So as long as he's home though with you things seem to be okay?

A: Yeah, yep. I guess *if I can survive until retirement, I'll be okay.* We'll be together all the time.

T: So you think if you can survive until retirement, he'll stop fooling around and get back to normal?

A: Yes, I think it will be okay. . . . Sometimes before he goes to work he just sits there with his eyes closed, because he can't look at me, he knows what he's doing. But he can't stop it I guess.

T: He feels guilty, but not enough to make him stop.

A: Right, and then sometimes he acts real arrogant about it, you know. Dad did that to Mom. Oh, poor old Mom. I just can't believe none of this.

T: It just doesn't make any sense.

A: Well, see, none of this business doesn't make sense. Just all the weird junk, it's awful. See, he's stubborn-headed. I told you he practically had to raise his self. This is what's made him. And probably its like a power thing, ya see what I'm saying to ya?

T: Uh-huh. Exactly. That's why he won't admit this.

A: I know, it's oh, it's denial.

T: He'll stop doing it when you retire, but I don't think he'd ever admit it to you.

A: Oh no, he won't never admit it. No, no, no.

T: And probably never will. But he may just give it up.

Commentary

The therapist continues to listen and admit Alice's observations as plausible. He does not question what her senses are telling her. Alice is aware that the therapist is interested in her account and not taking sides with her husband, despite what she perceives as her husband's attempt to win the therapist over. It is apparent, too, that Alice struggles with the failed legacy of her parent's marriage and fears the same for herself. The therapist remains attuned to this painful memory and in so doing helps legitimize Alice's anxiety.

In the conversation, the therapist learns that the weekends continue to affirm the relationship for the couple. What is more, Alice again marks an end to the problem after David retires. She will be okay, she says, if she can survive until the retirement. She offered this prospect herself.

The third session confirms that an alliance between Alice and the therapist has largely cemented. More important, Alice has established David's retirement as a terminating point for her worry—a connection has been discovered that opens a possibility for resolution of the client's dilemma. Until then, she only has to survive the wait. From our point of view, when the client can begin to identify both an ending to a problem and the actions needed to realize it, hope has been reestablished and resolution is on the way.

In the next meeting the therapist will listen for instances of Alice putting her emerging plan into effect.

SESSION FOUR

Excerpt One

T: So, how are you doing?

A: Oh, things are about the same, maybe a little better. I've been treating him better this week. A couple nights out of the week I don't sleep at first, but I just go on to sleep anyway. I finally got toughened up to it, I got mad and got toughened up to it. I'm sleeping better than I used to. But it's so hard to deal with. Then, I got P.O.'ed at him though, cause of the way he acted before he went to work, and he says, "You've been doing so good." Like it's all my fault.

T: That made you mad, didn't it?

A: Oh, I told him, "When are you going to do your share?" I said, "It all can't land on me."

T: That's right.

A: It all can't land on me, I can't do it. What I'd like to know is what is he doing with his money? This money is amounting into a lot of money. I don't know what the heck he's doing with it.

T: And your fear is that he's giving it to another woman.

A: He's either keeping somebody, or he's paying on that girl's car or something. I don't know what the heck he's doing with it. I'm getting tired of all this.

T: I don't blame you; it really gets old. So, one day since last Wednesday he's acted weird?

A: I know one day he did.

T: Okay, so maybe he's cut down a little bit?

A: Yea, I guess so. There was some black hairs in his undershorts one morning. I know this story sounds bizarre, it is, it does sound nuts.

T: Well, it is bizarre, but, that doesn't mean that it isn't true, though. A lot of people fool around on their spouses.

A: And we're getting closer to retirement. Okay, now! If he's keeping somebody, how in the heck does he expect to do this when we retire? There ain't no way he can afford to do this. But, I think we'll be okay after we're retired, I think he's got too much opportunity now.

T: Okay, so when he's retired, you'll be around each other a lot.

A: Right. That will fix most of this mess. We've got another month and something to go.

T: So the task is to figure out how to get through this five-week period. If he stays and nothing happens, you think you'll have a sense of relief once the retirement happens?

A: Yes.

T: Okay, let's be honest here a minute. You know he ain't going to admit it.

A: No, no. Are you kidding?

T: So, you're not holding on to that he's going to say: "I'm sorry, I've been messing around." He's never going to do any of that.

A: No way, he ain't never going to admit it, huh-uh! No, they can't do that. Dad was the same way. Dad would never admit nothing to Mom. They're denying it to their selves, not only to you, but to their selves that they're doing it. Oh, he's slick, man! And I'll tell you one thing: If I didn't love this man, I wouldn't have put up with this stuff.

T: No, you wouldn't.

A: I wouldn't put up with none of it!

T: No, you'd be gone already. What do you think would help you get through this next five-week period?

A: I don't know. I quit going around the neighborhood checking him out. I quit going down there around watching him. Although he's doing something. You know good and well if there's hairs on his undershorts, they're not on there for nothing.

T: Okay, but still, you've got to figure out a way to survive these five weeks, though. I mean, you've got to think of yourself, too.

A: If I've survived this long, I guess I can make it. I try to ignore some of it, but it's hard to do. But if we just make it to retirement, we'll be okay. But, the money's going someplace.

T: That's the biggest indicator to you.

A: Right now!

T: So, what's going to help you get through this? You've got five weeks to go before you'll have a lot more control, because he'll be around you a lot more. What's going to help you survive? You're a real survivor, Alice, there's no doubt about it. So, what's going to help you do that? You know he's not going to admit it. But, what can happen that will help you just get through the next five weeks? Think about that because let's try to hash out a game plan with David.

A: Okay.

T: Okay, that's going to be tough, now.

A: I don't care, I've been through so much; I don't care! You know? I just don't care . . . and I get tired thinking about it; I get tired dealing with it.

Commentary

Without instruction, coaching, or homework assignments, Alice has taken action to manage the five weeks until David's retirement. In her words, she "toughened up to it"; she enacts her intention to survive. In particular, she started treating David better and slept better at night. She stopped her surveillance. Maintaining her belief in her husband's infidelity, she also recognizes that he will stand by his assertion of innocence. He will not change his story. It is her love for David, she tells the therapist, that is seeing her through this crisis in the marriage and his denial.

The therapist takes no position on the wisdom of her decision to stay with her husband. It was her goal, put forth in the first session, for David to stop fooling around. This end, in her way of thinking, will become reality when he retires. She already has evidence, gathered on the weekends, that when he is with her, he is hers. The therapist abides by her goal.

We see Alice's decision to survive the time to retirement as an act of personal empowerment. Unilaterally, she took several steps to help herself and help the marriage. With this decision, she also took a step out of the victimization, be it real or imaginary, that helped keep her in the rut of doing more of the same.

What David is doing with the money (which Alice suspects he is squandering on the girlfriend), however, is still an issue. In the following session, the couple derives a way to settle it.

SESSION FIVE

Excerpt One

T: So, how are things going?

D: Oh, pretty good. Doing better.

T: Doing better?

D: I think so.

T: Okay, good. How come?

D: Well, she's not as nervous. Oh, she's not complained as much really.

T: Okay. That's real good. Not complaining as much, and not as nervous you think? Okay. [To Alice] How do you think things are going?

A: Oh well, they're going a little better, I guess.

T: Okay. And what makes you say that? What's going better, do you think?

A: Well, I've tried to treat him better than I was but it's not to say that, that he's changed his ways completely.

T: Umhm. Okay.

D: I don't know why you say I haven't changed my ways, I'm no different than I ever was.

T: You two have different positions about what's going on here. So, we all know that already and you're probably not going to convince one another that your way is right. And probably neither of you would admit it if you were wrong.

A: I might.

T: Okay.

D: That you was wrong?

A: Yes sir.

T: Okay. Well good, good. I'm glad you're that way. Given that you got different views about what's going on and I don't think you are going to convince one another that the other one's right, what I wanted to talk about was a plan you two could put together on how you're going to get through the next five weeks before you retire, David. Alice was telling me that she thought everything would be okay if she could just get through to when you retired. Okay, so, what I wanted to talk about was what needs to happen between you two to get through from now until when you retire.

Commentary

A symmetrical struggle to settle the question of whose version of reality is correct has already served no one. The therapist endeavors to delimit that unproductive solution. Curiously, Alice interjects that she would be willing to concede error. Yet, considering the moment in which she makes this surprising offer, there is danger of igniting another round of argument should the therapist pursue it. It is almost as though she is saying to David, "By willing to admit I was wrong, I'm the better person for it." As such, the therapist makes the judgment call to stay with and fine-tune what is working. Given the intensity of their ongoing disagreement, he reasons that any apologies or concessions might better come later, especially when they can land on less acrimonious soil. On the other hand, given the benefit of hindsight, Alice's comment may have been a forcast of things to come that could have been unfolded and expanded.

Excerpt Two

D: I mean, good Lord, she gets in her head that I'm doing this and I'm doing this. I don't know how you're going to get it out of her head that I'm not doing this.

T: I'm not trying to get it out of her head. I'm trying to have you two work a solution out that you both can live with until you retire. That may take a lot of the pressure off, once you retire. [To Alice] What would you like David to do differently than he's doing now?

A: If you'd quit doing what you're doing, then things would be fine. I'm trying to be better to you but therefore you have got to cooperate. I'd like for him to quit putting a hundred dollars out of his check every week some place.

T: Okay. Now how can he demonstrate to you that he's not doing that?

A: I don't know.

T: That's the kinds of things we've got to come up with. If you're going to be able to state what you want, David has got to be able to show that he's doing that. So, that's what we need to hammer out. Unless that happens you two are going to be at odds for the next five weeks and that's a long time when you're having a lot of discomfort.

D: Yeah. I've offered to, to sign my check, I've offered to give it to her. No, she won't take it.

T: So if David signed his check over to you, he brought his check intact and signed it over to you, would that help the money issue?

A: Just as long as I knew he's not doing something with a hundred dollars of his check, it'd make a big difference in what's going on.

T: So how can he demonstrate to you that he's not doing that?

Okay, so if you took the check, would that be a way to handle that issue? Would that be a way for David to demonstrate that he's not spending that money elsewhere?

A: Yes, but I hate to think that I have to go to these kind of measures.

T: Well, we're looking at measures between now and when David retires. These are drastic measures to get you through the period between now and then. So sometimes you've got to do drastic things to get through a bad period of time.

A: It's not to say that he just won't go somewhere else to get the money.

T: Well, how can that be addressed?

D: Well, if I go to the credit union we always get a statement if there's any money drawn out. Or she can call or look at my check stub for the balance.

T: So if you started looking at the credit union statements you would know whether David was taking money out. Because you would have that information. You would have his check stub, you would also have all the information from the credit union.

A: Right. And then when he retires then all the money's going in together and, and we'll both see that things gets paid and do what we want to do. We've already talked all that out.

T: You're just talking about the next five weeks this will have to be. So is that an agreement then?

A: Is that an agreement, Dad, or not?

D: Fine with me.

Commentary

In this segment, the therapist successfully redirects the couple's attention to a plan for survival. The goal is not to change their marriage forever, but to reach agreement, lasting at least the next five weeks, on what they can do to bridge the gap that has divided them. Making the plan time-limited is designed to help ensure their participation.

At this stage, the therapist emphasizes sticking to specifics and doing what is do-able. Alice goes for tackling the money question. The therapist assumes the role of mediator. After arriving at a plan for managing the money, other outstanding issues are approached.

Excerpt Three

T: So that's the money part, now what about the other part? Tell me what else would help get you through?

D: As long as this lady thinks I'm fooling around, she ain't gonna get no better.

A: Let me tell you something. If I was doing what you're doing, do you think you'd stick with me?

D: But Alice. I'm telling you, we've been trying to tell you, I'm not doing this stuff.

A: Some of this stuff I know you did.

T: I don't think it will help to try to talk her out of her beliefs of what's going on. Okay. Try to address what she needs from you to help her get through this time period. And then she'll either believe you or not believe you. Don't focus your time on trying to talk her out of it. I just don't think that's helpful. I haven't seen where that's gotten you anywhere. [To Alice] What else would help you get through this period of time before David retires?

A: I just wish he'd quit sneaking around doing what he's doing. You can always tell when he's up to something. He's either gets stuff, he puts it in his [car] trunk because he's gotta do stuff for these women. It makes him feel better about hisself.

T: So if he lets you know what he's doing, like if he puts something in his trunk and he tells you what he's doing. That would help you if he gave you more information about what he was doing? That would help you get through this next time period?

A: Yeah. The thing of it is that I've told you this before now like on the weekends he's fine. But then you get ready to go back to work things changes. Now just like this week we'll be off, we'll be fine. Okay.

T: Okay. So what else can David do? You only got a few more weeks and like you said things are fine on the weekends when you're around each other. Like next week on the vacation, things will be good between you. So you really have a few weeks of time here that you gotta plod through this mess. So what's going to help you two through that period of time?

D: Yeah, what do I need to, what do you want me to do? I can't stay home. I gotta go to work.

T: [To David] "What can I do to make this easier on you? What do I need to do to allow you to see that I'm not fooling around? What can I do in this situation to make it better for you?" Ask her what you need to do to help her feel better and focus it on that. And whatever she says, if you can do it, do it.

A: What I'd like to know is are you really interested in saving the marriage?

D: I've always told you there wouldn't be no divorce. There ain't going to never be no divorce.

A: But you see we can't live this way. We can't live this way from now on. It's been hell.

D: I'll agree to that.

T: So what's going to help during that time period when David's getting ready to go to work? What do you want to see from him? Alice, what's going to help?

A: I'd like for you to be the same way every day before you leave. I'd just like seeing him relax before he goes. That's all. Whelp, he says he's here to save the marriage as much as I am. Right?

D: That's what we're here for.

A: I'll try if he will. I've been trying. He's got to say that I've done better. I'm fine till something happens. See, if he was open with me about things, if it was just a friend of his that needed something done and he told me, that'll be a whole different ballgame. But you see he's not including me in none of this. So therefore I make, maybe I make more out of this than what's going on, but he wouldn't want me at some man's house cooking his meals and taking care of him and everything. I'll say maybe I jump to conclusions sometimes, but you see you made me this way. You're the one that made me this way. But, we'll be fine when we're off, when he retires.

Commentary

True to her earlier statement, Alice does admit her part in the couple's difficulties. This is a significant development. Not only has she connected the resolution of her dilemma to a forseeable future, Alice has also revised her perspective to include the possibility that David is not having an affair. This, we believe, is a testament to her openness and flexibility, as well as the power of validation. Let's retrace the progression of events.

With the therapist's mediation, the couple continues to work out an arrangement. At times, the therapist models a method of negotiation, instructs, and mildly confronts the couple on the need to continue to do something different with each other. In using a more active and directive role, the therapist is relying on the alliance. The couple agree they are here to preserve the marriage. They are now bargaining the interim steps that are needed to facilitate that goal. The therapist uses his relationship, his bond, with the couple to help nudge them gently, and at the same time, forcefully, in the direction they want to go. They accept his input and work together, a further confirmation of the alliance.

This conjoint segment ends with Alice concluding that perhaps she has been jumping to conclusions and making more out of David's behavior than might be warranted. She saves face, though, by also saying that David made her this way. Clearly, she is ready to stand down from her stance, but she will not capitulate.

This is a delicate development in the couple's relationship and the therapist decides to pursue the importance of this event with David individually. In this way, he can underscore its significance without: (a) embarrassing Alice or (b) forcing her to withdraw her concession if she feels David is using it to let himself off the hook.

Excerpt Four

T: She said two things today that she's never said before. She said, "Maybe I jump to conclusions" and "Maybe I make more out of it than what it really is."

D: Yeah.

T: She's not said that before to me. It's still bad for you right now, but I'm saying that's major progress. Because she's starting to challenge it a little bit herself. But you gotta really work hard on not being defensive.

D: Whew!

T: I know you wanna respond with righteous indignation because you know you're innocent. But you know that's not going to help. She made two comments today, though that was the first I'd heard of it. That's the first indication she's given at all that any of it is her own part. Was that the first time you heard that stuff?

D: Yeah. That's the first time I've heard that.

T: Okay, so I realize that it's not fast. She's not getting better real quick. And it's not like she is going to wake up one day and say, "You're right, I've been crazy all along." She ain't gonna do that.

D: She ain't never gonna admit it.

T: No. No, she's not.

D: Oh man, I swear. Whew. This is really hard.

T: Well it hurts you bad to think that she thinks that about you. That is really tough to deal with.

D: What's it gonna take, years?

T: I don't know, but I don't think so. You all have been coming here for about 8 weeks.

D: Yes.

T: And there's already a change. I think the retirement's gonna make a big difference. She's better on the weekends when you're around her. As long as you don't keep trying to get her to admit that she's wrong.

Commentary

The therapist uses this time alone with David to punctuate the importance of what has happened. In addition, as the team has suggested, he works hard to join with the client around his frustration and impatience. The therapist wants to ensure that David will no longer resort to attacking Alice's perceptions and protesting his innocence—going back to "more of the same." One might see this time as a good-natured coaching, "Hang in there, you're close to winning. Stay on track and don't blow it."

In the next and last session, the couple's progress is assessed first with Alice alone and then with the couple.

SESSION SIX

Excerpt One

A: I saw his problem on TV. And he's going through exactly what they say these men go through. He's a completely changed person from what he use to be and that's what these men do. It's nothing they can help. He feels sorry that he's not the man he use to be, and that is a bunch of baloney. So therefore he keeps trying to convince hisself by doing all this stuff for women, to make him feel good about hisself. I try telling him he's no different in that way. So therefore he just hurting hisself and our marriage is what he's doing. Trying to convince hisself that he's not. Men go through a change just like the women. I kept trying to tell him that but he wouldn't listen. And that's exactly what this is. It's the hormones. Men has one kind of hormones, women have another. Women, when they go through the change, their estrogen goes down. So they have problems. The men has this other. I got it wrote in my purse. Testosterone. And it goes down. If he would just accept the change.

T: Well I think he's trying to. You have noticed that he's trying.

A: Yeah, I have.

T: So, how do you think it's going?

A: It's better, we just got two weeks left. I'm not saying he's completely better, but I think he's cutting back.

T: You think this thing is running its course and he is coming to his senses?

A: I think so. Is that possible?

T: I think so. Especially since he knows that you are on to him, and he won't have any opportunity anymore. And maybe he's learned from this whole mess what he needed to learn, that he should just retire and spend the rest of his life with you.

A: Well, I hope so. I do think we are going to make it now.

Commentary

Alice shares her etiological hunch about David's alleged infidelity. She apparently is looking for an explanation for his behavior and hormones could provide an answer. Not surprising, we learn from her that David is no more eager to accept this interpretation than any contrary to his own. True to his purpose of steadfastly avoiding the role of reality's arbiter, the therapist sidesteps Alice's remark and comes back to what is working. His intent is not to ignore her, but simply to avoid discussions that are more of the same. This is the road to impossibility that the couple wants less traveled.

On questioning, Alice acknowledges David's efforts. She also agrees, with appropriate caution, that they have turned the problem around. The final segment follows.

Excerpt Two

T: David, how do you think it's going?

D: Better. We had a great vacation. She seemed like her old self. She didn't get nervous and she didn't bring any of this stuff up. She never mentioned the money again. She is sleeping better too. I think we're both more relaxed.

A: Well, you didn't do anything for me to get nervous about. Like, I said, maybe I do jump to conclusions sometimes, but I had good reason. I just ain't had no reason lately. We spent a lot of time just talking about retirement and what we was going to do. That helped.

T: How did that help?

A: I felt for the first time in a long time that we was actually going to have a retirement together, because I was afraid that I was going to wind up like my mom.

D: I ain't never going to leave you.

A: I believe that.

Commentary

Alice repeats her concession of jumping to conclusions and still holds David responsible for her behavior. While one might look for the couple to profess their mistakes and seek forgiveness, under the circumstances Alice has made a major move. It should not be minimized. In addition, it looks like David will not be as forthcoming, but perhaps by pledging his commitment he is attempting to meet his wife halfway. We never knew whether David was having an affair.

About six months later, Alice enclosed a postcard with her final payment. The card said:

Enjoying our retirement very much. We love our home in the mountains and the fresh air. David don't miss going to the shop every day. David seems to have come to his senses and accepted the change and all. But that don't mean that I'm not keeping an eye on him. I appreciated your keeping an open mind and not letting David pull one over on me.

DISCUSSION

Certainly, the question of whether David was actually having an affair has direct bearing on Alice's diagnosis of delusional disorder. As noted, we were not able to establish that finding. Prior providers were apparently convinced of Alice's psychosis and attempted to treat her as such. David, whether dissimulating or not, also labeled his wife as disturbed.

From the beginning, the stance was to remove ourselves from the recruitment of the diagnosis and the former helpers' interventions. We saw that attempting to induce Alice into a patient role had become a sure pathway to impossibility. Exhortations, psychoeducation, or medication brought relief for neither Alice nor David. Something else was needed.

As with the other cases in this volume, the alliance was a major order of business. We also saw that the couple was in a stubborn standoff, assured of their positions and not about to back down. In the words of Fisch et al. (1982), the couple was trapped in "confirming the accuser's suspicions by defending oneself" (p. 155). The task was to find a way to join with the couple, honor and accommodate their frames of reference, block the reciprocal incriminations, enable their motivation to preserve the marriage, and identify new possibilities for action.

Validation proved to be the therapist's best friend in working with Alice. The indignity and invalidation she experienced prior yielded when she was regarded as a competent woman with a right to her own interpretations and perceptions. Finding that she was not going to be regarded as a kook or pariah, she slowly began to identify her own ideas for resolution.

The more the therapist believed her, and believed in her, the more open Alice became to letting go of the aspects of her "delusional jealousy" that were not helpful. Surviving to retirement became her connection to possibility, her theory of changing her troubling circumstance. The therapist honored that theory and collaborated with Alice and David to see them through to retirement.

In working with David, moreover, his commitment to Alice proved therapeutic. Alice was terrified of a repetition of her mother's life. When David assured her he would stay, he provided a needed affirmation. This act helped to eject the conflict from their lives.

In this case, the therapist might be accused of agreeing with the client's "delusion." To repeat, we had no knowledge one way or another that David was unfaithful. As a result, as much as we knew, Alice could be dead right. Yet, going to David and confronting him about his behavior, in our opinion, was not a viable intervention. Alice had become an expert in confrontation with him, all to no avail. To repeat what was not working made no sense.

In comparing our work with other treatments of delusional disorder, we saw no recourse in medication. Alice was agitated—she was crying and pacing the floor and not sleeping. For all that, psychopharmacotherapy was attempted and Alice did not comply. In agreement with other therapies, we saw our work as supportive. That is, we supported the clients' frames of reference and had an unswerving faith in their eventual ability to circumvent their conflict and reach a measure of accord.

Looking back, we were moved by this case. The reported power of delusions was not lost on us and we were delighted with the couple's success. More important, we were touched by Alice's resilience. She stayed true to her perceptions, did not back down, and yet was also ready to take advantage of possibility as the pathways to impossibility were removed and her theory of change was honored.

CHAPTER 8

Case Example: Borderline Personality Disorder or "What's Wrong with Me?"

People are generally better persuaded by the reasons which they have themselves discovered than by those which have come into the minds of others.

Pascal

THIS CHAPTER PRESENTS the treatment of a diagnostic mainstay of the mental health industry, borderline personality disorder (BPD). Probably no other diagnosis strikes fear in the hearts of therapists, or evokes cold chills like BPD. A brief review of treatment recommendations for BPD is presented, inviting the reader to continue to compare traditional approaches to the one offered in this book. Excerpted dialogue and commentary will illustrate our approach as well as illuminate the particular pathways to impossibility that Jay, the veteran whose treatment is under scrutiny in this chapter, traveled. Jay provides a provocative example of how a theory-driven approach—in this case a solution-oriented validation of client competence—can go awry when such actions do not attend to client motivations and honor the client's theory of change.

BORDERLINE PERSONALITY DISORDER: TREATMENT RECOMMENDATIONS

Overview

With the recent and possible exception of multiple personality disorder, no condition has more captured the attention, and perhaps

154

imagination, of therapists than borderline personality disorder. In professional conferences and informal conversations, anxious war stories are told and retold, giving rise to the legend of the impossible borderline patient. The customary characterizations include impulsiveness, affective instability, hostile dependency, and dangerousness—features which can readily intimidate the most stolid of clinicians.

Despite the voluminous literature describing the borderline personality, from etiology to psychopathology to treatment, much remains poorly understood. Confident, theoretically-derived explanations abound, but few reliable facts exist. The therapy of the condition is complicated by the diversity of opinion regarding what even to call borderline.

In actual practice, the term was often used to denote an untreatable patient in psychoanalytic treatment, the so-called latent schizophrenic, or as a derogatory and prejudicial trash can grouping for people who defied categorization and clinical management. Modern nosology offers little clarity. Within the *DSM-III* and *III-R*, using five or more of the eight criteria, there are 93 possible ways to arrive at the diagnosis (Beutler & Clarkin, 1990). The *DSM-IV* (American Psychiatric Association, 1994) provides for five out of nine.

In addition, good epidemiological data establishing the breadth of the disorder are not available. Estimates place its prevalence within 2 to 4 percent in normal populations, with a much higher presence, between 15 and 25 percent, in clinical settings. Women are disproportionately represented in this classification, accounting for two-thirds or more of the patients diagnosed. The borderline is said to be the most common form of personality disorder (Gunderson, 1989).

The imperfect understanding of BPD has not dampened enthusiasm for treating it. To date, "the cornerstone of most treatments" is individual psychotherapy (Gunderson, 1989, p. 1394). A concise discussion of that therapy approach as well as other principal strategies follows.

Individual Psychotherapy

The psychoanalytic community has been productive not only in richly hypothesizing the genesis of BPD, but also recommending the necessary parameters for individual therapy. Though their impact has been keenly felt, particularly in popularizing the diagnosis, they remain divided as to what elements of an individual therapy are most needed.

One school says that the treatment should emphasize an exploratory insight-orientation (e.g., Kernberg, Selzer, Koenigsberg, Carr, & Appelbaum, 1987). Proponents of this model maintain the presumed aggression, hostility, and manipulation of the client with BPD require early confrontation and interpretation. In contrast, advocates of what may be described as a supportive approach to therapy stress creating the conditions in which an alliance can develop (e.g., Zetzel, 1971). Imputing hostile motives to the client's behavior is avoided in favor of helping the client to feel understood. Both traditions report success, but their comparative value has not been established (Gunderson, 1989).

Aside from psychoanalytically-informed therapy, interpersonal, behavioral, and cognitive treatments have recently been directed to BPD. The effectiveness of these approaches has yet to reach a firm empirical base (Shea, 1991).

Linehan and colleague's (e.g., Koerner & Linehan, 1992) "dialectical behavior therapy" conceptualizes the problems of the client as deficiencies in adaptive behavior and excesses of maladaptive behavior. The therapy seeks to expand the client's capabilities and skills. Character change or understandings of etiology or "psychodynamic concomitants" are not targeted. To participate in the therapy, the client agrees to (a) decrease life-threatening behavior, (b) decrease interpersonal behaviors that interfere with treatment as well as those that undermine quality of life (e.g., substance abuse, losing housing), and (c) increase behavioral skills. Once progress is realized on these goals, the focus turns to reducing the enduring effects of childhood physical and sexual abuse, "then to development of broad-based self-respect, and finally work toward any other client goals" (Koerner & Linehan, 1992, p. 442). Results with this approach are mixed, though some data suggest that the therapy may show promise in reducing self-destructive actions (Hollon & Beck, 1994).

Currently, guidelines for the individual therapy of BPD include providing structure, consistency, support, and limit-setting for the client (Chessick, 1993; Johnson, 1991). The therapy is expected to be protracted, tedious, and taxing of the therapist's emotions and patience, yielding uneven results. Considerable experience is recommended in working with the client or in the absence of the necessary experience, supervision (Gunderson, 1989).

Psychopharmacotherapy

Brinkley (1993) asserts that the knowledge base supporting the pharmacological treatment of BPD—at an early stage of development—is only marginally exceeded by our ability to define the nosological limits of the disorder. Trial and error seems to be the rule in prescriptive practice. Neuroleptics, antidepressants, lithium carbonate, carbamazepine, and benzodiazepines have been used to manage the cognitive, emotional, impulsive-behavioral, and anxious-fearful symptoms that are thought to typify borderline functioning. According to Soloff (1994), results support acute treatment; maintenance trials are few and show only narrow effectiveness.

In all, the data suggest that available drug therapy has an unimpressive record of efficacy with BPD (Rosenberg, 1994). No single drug treatment of choice exists (Soloff, 1994). Hope is placed in future research. For example, Rosenberg argues that progress in neuroscience, particularly in the area of the psychobiology of personality, may benefit medication approaches.

Group and Family Therapy

Group therapies are regarded to be helpful with BPD. Notwithstanding, owing to clients' apparent inability to share attention with others and weather confrontation, group therapy is frequently conducted along with individual therapy. What is more, individual therapy is often made contingent on group participation (Gunderson, 1989).

Clarkin, Marziali, and Munroe-Blum (1991), in their review of clinical and empirical studies of group and family treatments for BPD, cite support for the use of a group format. They note, though, that no study has tested whether group treatment sequenced or combined with individual therapy, or individual treatment alone, is better than group therapy alone. Further, although mentioning a rational basis for the use of family therapy, the reviewers point to the lack of research investigating this intervention modality with BPD clients.

Conclusion

"Treatment of borderline patients with medication, psychotherapy, or both is problematic" (Beitman, Hall, & Woodward, 1992,

p. 546). This conclusion summarizes what even the most casual survey of the literature reveals. Specifying effective treatments for BPD of whatever stripe continues to be undermined by the fuzziness of the category and by the often observed tendency to invoke the label in the face of provocative or difficult clinical presentations. In our experience, therapy veterans, given their typical history of "treatment failure," become especially vulnerable to being assigned the BPD diagnosis.

Because of the imprecision surrounding the field's understanding of those ultimately called borderline, clinicians have little more to go on than well-intentioned advice and clinical lore. A recurring theme in the writings is that therapists can expect hard-going with the client. Additionally, it is suggested that the treatment should include firm limits on the client's dependency strivings and manipulative attempts to extort attention. One might form the impression from the literature that therapists should place themselves in the role of a parent, authoritatively dispensing structure and restraint to manage an unruly child.

THE CASE OF JAY

Jay was referred for consultation by Carrie, a talented therapist well-known for her solution-focused (Berg & Miller, 1992; de Shazer, 1994), validation-based (Duncan et al., 1992) approach. After six sessions, she was concerned that little, if any, progress was being made. The client agreed that the problem situation was only becoming more frustrating. According to the therapist, sessions revolved unendingly around ideas that never seemed to take hold and result in change ("His statements of contradiction were so numerous my head was spinning"). Sessions usually concluded with intense emotional pleadings from the client, agonizingly begging for help and hope. The experience left the therapist reeling with exasperation.

Jay, truly a veteran of misery in many ways, had a horrendous story to tell, a story that painted a vivid picture of emotional abuse, rejection, abandonment, unresolved issues with his father, low self-esteem, and shame. Jay's emotional turmoil had led him to a string of physicians, psychologists, support groups, etc., only to find that each quickly passed him off to other helpers, or suggested that since he could identify his problems, he could handle them on his own.

The referring therapist learned that the intensity of Jay's emotions evoked several diagnoses from previous helpers, such as BPD, dependent personality disorder, and, according to one psychiatrist, even delusional disorder.

However, the diagnosis that seemed to recur was that Jay was a "functional" borderline. It is indeed paradoxical that Jay carried such serious diagnoses while simultaneously persuading previous helpers to dismiss him for not having anything wrong with him. It seemed that no one wanted to deal with his intensity. Jay's greatest fear was that he would be told again that there was nothing wrong with him that he could not fix on his own.

According to the referring therapist, during the first six therapy sessions, true to her competence-based style, she was careful to stay clear of the attribution creep and validated Jay's experiences of a horrendous past. Indeed, looking at the long list of hurts and disappointments in Jay's life, it was truly amazing that he was so successful. Carrie also saw Jay as being motivated, resourceful, and willing to work. According to the therapist, each time she validated his competencies and focused on strengths to address his distress, Jay seemed to become more upset and would respond with "What's wrong with me?"

The therapist tried to accommodate the client's desire to "be fixed" by working with his many resources. She searched for exceptions and validated his competence; Jay continued to feel hopeless and frustrated, was still in turmoil, and was becoming desperate. The end-of-session emotional storms had become intolerable to the therapist. At this point Carrie responsibly called for help for this "impossible case." Jay agreed to be seen by the team and was interviewed for two sessions by one of the authors. Carrie participated on the team.

SESSION ONE

Excerpt One

T: This is kind of a strange process, so it might take a couple of minutes to get used to a group behind the mirror observing. What will happen is we'll talk for about forty-five minutes, and then we'll take a break. Then I'll go back behind the mirror and talk with the team and see if they have any suggestions or feedback they want to give you, and then I'll come back and share that with you.

J: Right.

T: I may get a phone call or two while we're in here so if the phone rings it is for me [both laugh], so I'll answer it and I'll share what they say or what they want me to ask. So, what will be helpful for us to hear is what is bringing you here to see me?

J: I have to work into my mood because I spend so much of my time really hiding my feelings. There are very few people out there that can really see through me. One of those is my wife. A lot of this started last March when my father passed away. There was some unresolved expectations or needs or hurts or whatever there was with him that I apparently didn't know I had until he passed on, and now they never will be resolved. At first I thought they were just normal grieving processes, but the needs became more intense and I knew there was more to it. I allowed myself to go through the grieving process. I expressed my emotions to my wife and other people, but they just continued on.

T: Uh-huh.

J: I realized I was hurting those people that cared for me most. My wife is like a sponge . . . She can't take any more. She doesn't know what to do to help. I am hurting her. There are a lot of emotions that need to come out. There is something bothering me and I don't know what it is . . . and I refuse . . . here we go [voice trembling and tears forming] . . . I refuse to give up and that's why I came back again to therapy. I am not going to let these hurts . . . I'm not going to let these emotions . . . I'm not going to repress anymore. I'm going to let them through. It's too easy to just repress them. And there's hurt there; the tears keep swelling up and I don't know what it is!

T: Okay, sounds like you are going through a lot.

J: I don't know how far you want me to go back. Want me to go back and name things that hurt in my childhood?

T: That would be fine. I would be interested in what you think it could be that is bothering you.

J: I want to be liked. I want to be needed, not to say my wife and children aren't giving me those things, but apparently it's not enough. I don't know what I want [getting louder, voice breaking]; I don't know what's wrong!

T: Okay, you just can't put your finger on it—what's wrong with you.

J: I don't know. From my conversations with Carrie, I am a sensitive person, maybe to the ultra extreme. I read some of my grandmother's writing, and it may be a character trait or something that can be handed down that is, this sensitivity thing, and I've never learned how to handle it. And that is what I'm trying to identify. Because, if it is a trait or a problem, let's identify it and let's learn how to go about handling it or retraining me. Can that be done after 40-some years? Can I retrain patterns that have been ingrained 40 years? That is a question.

T: I think it can happen.

J: And I see these traits happening in my son. I wish I would listen to myself like he listens to me. Why can't I listen to myself?

T: That's a good question.

J: I'm hurting on the inside and I don't know why; I can't figure it out.

Commentary

The consulting therapist began with the assumption that Jay's desires for treatment had not been addressed. Consequently, he intended to focus on Jay's goals as a first order of business. Because of Carrie's experience, the team had taken care to cultivate a beginner's mind. It took only a short time for the team to appreciate the intensity of Jay's presentation. Jay quickly identified an issue of great importance to him, namely, finding out what is wrong with him. Also apparent were many strengths (e.g., strong relationship with wife, ability to help son), but given Carrie's experience with validating strengths and the significance of the client's pursuit of what's wrong with him, the consulting therapist refrained from comment. Note that the client did not respond to or even acknowledge supportive/validating comments (e.g., "Sounds like you are going through a lot"). This is not a criticism of the client or the therapist, but rather an observation that the team noticed. Monitoring the client's response enables therapists to let go of approaches or styles that do not obtain the desired results. The therapist moves to explore the client's perceptions of what is wrong, looking for the client's theory to emerge, hoping to create a context for the discovery of possibilities that may open a pathway out of the client's dilemma.

Excerpt Two

T: Do you have any other ideas about that? You mentioned that one of the things that you identify is your sensitivity. Is there any other thing that you can point to?

J: Yeah, if we just start back in my childhood, I'll give you my autobiography. First grade . . . I had to repeat first grade because I had a lazy eye and they didn't feel I had learned enough to go on because I couldn't see the board correctly. I took a lot of ridicule from my classmates because of that. I was doing fairly well in school until I hit the fifth grade; a teacher totally demoralized me. And that really hurt me a lot. I failed out of junior high, altogether. At that time I was seeing a child psychologist. They wanted to identify what is wrong and I took lots of tests, I can't remember all the tests. I remember drawing pictures for the doctor, putting blocks together, ink blot test, like that. I had a brain wave scan and stuff like that. I had no idea what it was for, but I did it.

T: Uh-huh.

J: They took me out of the public school system and put me into a school for kids of special needs . . . for retards, and I was immediately assigned that label, a "retard." And I was called that by the neighborhood kids and by my brother and sister [starting to cry again].

T: What a tragic legacy. Gosh.

J: My dad did not want me to graduate from that high school. So, they took me from that school, threw me back into a public high school. And of course, I carried that retard title with me through public school system. I came out with a low B average. But, I didn't have any friends; the kids in the neighborhood would not play with me. I associated with my brother's friends. And the reason, I was told later, was they let me do that because my brother was there. They didn't want to play with me. I carry a lead mark on my hand where they held it out and took a pencil and just put it right into my hand, like that [demonstrates], and I still carry that piece of lead to this day. One day they jumped me and hog-tied my hands behind my back and left rope burns on my arms [sobbing, takes a minute to collect himself].

T: Cruel kids.

J: My own brother and his friends. I left home to go to a tech school. I was totally unprepared for life when I went up there. I moved in with a bunch of roommates. And, of course, beer started flowing, women started flowing. I wasn't into that type of stuff. I was asked if I was gay, because I didn't have women up to the apartment to sleep with. I went through two sets of roommates because of that. I couldn't conform to that. It wasn't me. I left and moved in with a good friend of mine. He just recently got married and bought this house. And, he needed someone to rent the third bedroom out. Things went well there, except I lost my job with a shoe store. Told I wasn't management material and they laid me off. I asked what they meant by that, but they didn't explain.

T: Uh-huh.

J: I went to the Army and within six months my good friend and his wife got a divorce. She was cheating on him. What was going on while I was in the house? So, immediately eyes were drawn to me, that I was having an affair with her, which was not the case. While I was in the Army, I had a girlfriend, that just after a couple of months said, "I'm leaving." "Why?" "Well, if you don't know I'm certainly not telling you." And then she just took off. What's wrong with me [pleading]?

T: She didn't give you any answer to that?

J: Nah, she didn't give any answer to that. And, another girlfriend, while I was in the Army, she also left me. She just didn't know how to handle me and my emotions. Rather than deal with me or work through it, she just left me. Well, then I met my wife. One time, we weren't even going out seriously, we were part of the same group and we all met together on Sunday night. Well I took a seat and she goes and sits with someone else. Now, I had to leave; I just had to go home and I couldn't go to work the next morning. I was so emotionally bothered by that. Why? I don't understand what need was there. But I knew I was upset. I went home and cried for the next day. Why was there hurt there? Why was that need to the point that it caused that reaction inside of me?

But the other thing about that situation is I had many fears because of that girl in the Army that left me. She said the reason she fell in love with me was because of the way I treated her. No guy had ever treated her like that before. I treated her like a woman. I held the door open for her. I teased her with flowers. I gave her a rose with a little note. So this girl who dumped me was never treated like that by a guy, with courtesy and respect, so she says she fell in love with me. We were talking engagement and marriage. Because of the way I treated her, not for being myself or at least that's what she said the reason was. I bring that point up because my wife said the same thing to me before that night at the meeting. She said she liked me for the way I treated her. And I thought, oh, I just did this once before and got dumped. I'm doing it again, guess who's going to get dumped again! So, I was very upset when my to-be wife wouldn't sit by me.

T: Uh-huh.

J: See, I didn't date in high school. No one would go out with me. I remember having a girl, I liked her, this was before the girl who dumped me or my wife. So, she said let's go out for a drive. Of course that just kicked in the hormones. But before anything happened, she just opened up about how her father beat her as a child and how she wore leg braces as a child. It just totally blew me away, that she said all these things to me. So, I counseled her several times. I talked to her about her feelings, what she's going through, and stuff like that. So, she ended up marrying my boss. Hurt, but people seek me out . . .

T: As a confidant.

J: Yeah. And that happened several times with women and that hurt. That hurts a lot.

T: Kind of a double-edge sword. In one sense, there's something very positive about it, but in another sense, there's something very cutting and hurtful about that.

J: And I don't mind helping people out. I think that's a gift or a special intuition. But I can't help myself. And quite honestly I feel extremely discouraged that I'm sitting here in front of half a dozen people behind the mirror to find out what am I doing wrong. Why does it take six people to figure out what's wrong with me?

T: Human beings are complex creatures . . . Jay, although they are there, I'm not going to comment on your strengths and your insights because that's not why you are here. You're here to try to find out what's wrong. So, I am curious to know what other people have told you about what's wrong with you?

J: They wouldn't.

T: They wouldn't tell you what's wrong with you?

J: They say, "Jay, you are a neat person." I say, "Why do you say that?" "Oh, you just are."

T: Okay, they really wouldn't cut to the chase and give you the truth.

J: A neighbor, who also works with me, we have become fairly close friends. We went on a trip on an intensive project. I don't know what I said to her, I don't know what I did to her, but she could not talk to me or face me for several months after we got back. She was totally burned out. Here's a person whom I work for, who can see me for who I am in the work relationship in meetings and other arenas. Who I thought would be open and honest enough because of the friendship to tell me what's going on, to tell me honest feedback. But, she couldn't do it. And I wish I'd never done that to her.

T: Okay, okay.

J: I tried taking close people who I could trust aside and no one will give me an answer.

T: About what's wrong with you?

J: Right, they wouldn't give me anything. See that's what's bothering me.

T: Okay, it's bothering you that you can't get honest feedback from

people. Your friends aren't telling you what's wrong with you.
Have your counselors identified what's wrong with you?

J: You don't want to hear about that. My doctor, my physical
doctor said, "You need to go see a psychologist." So, one of the
other counseling groups around here called me back on the
phone. They said, "We don't really think you need to come in,
you need to go to a support group." So, I went to the support
group and they said, "No, we really can't help you out, you need
to go back to your psychologist or back to your doctors." I went
to a different psychologist and she said all that was wrong was
that I was overreacting and needed to change the way I look at
things. I didn't think she was right. If I am overreacting, where is
all this emotion coming from? She also referred me to a psychiatrist who prescribed some medicine, but I didn't see the point in
that. He said it would help me calm down and think. I can think
just fine. How can a medicine tell me what's wrong with me? It's
just a big brush-off. So, doctors say go here, they say go here,
they tell me nothing is really wrong other than the way I think
about things, and it's back to square one again.

T: Ping-Pong ball.

J: Ping-Pong, yeah, and I'm tired of people telling me, "You have a
good head on your shoulders. You seem to know what to tell
other people. You just need to trust in yourself, and listen to
yourself, and to have a good day." I don't want to hear that
[emphatically]. I'm scared of hearing it from this group, too
[beginning to cry].

T: Because that gives you nothing.

J: That gives me nothing. So, I have talked to other counselors.
And no one gives me any feedback [crying, getting louder and
emphatic]. No one will tell me what's going on!

T: Okay, and you have gotten that package answer from everyone
you talk to, that you have a good head on your shoulders, good
insight, and you just need to trust in your feelings.

J: Right, because people don't want to mess with me.

T: No one wants to mess with you, to take the time to figure out
what's going on and identify what the situation is. And that's
really frustrating and hurtful to you because you want to get

something going for yourself, because you know there's something wrong. [Pause] We need to take a break. I would like to ask one more question before we do that. Is there a particular example that comes to your mind that illustrates this thing that is wrong with you that would help us understand?

J: I have this desire to be wanted or needed. I walk into the mall and the first thing I know this woman is touching me on the shoulder and kidding and stuff like that. That's a need. I will find myself going back to those people and talking to them again. I'm feeling something inside of me. And I don't know what it is. I want to be wanted.

T: Okay. And is this an example of what is wrong with you, the need to be wanted?

J: I don't know.

T: Okay.

J: I'm just exhibiting symptoms. But, there's a root cause. And all I have been expressing is symptoms.

T: Okay. So, you are interested in the cause, the root cause.

J: I want to find the root cause and not just treat the symptom.

Commentary

The therapist explored Jay's world and the client told his story of multiple rejections by parents, siblings, teachers, girlfriends, co-workers, and even professional helpers. The exploration of "solution attempts" and what others had told him allowed Jay to articulate his bottom-line concern: He was afraid no one cared enough to "mess" with him. No one would give him an answer. Exploring Jay's world also allowed the discovery of what Jay was looking for from therapy: to find the root cause of his distress. That, therefore, must be what therapy gives him if it is to work. The consulting therapist and the team observed a notable difference in Jay's response when the therapist's comments reflected an appreciation of Jay's desire to find out what's wrong.

The first step in creating an efficient therapeutic encounter with psychotherapy veterans is to assume that therapy has failed to understand and address their desires. It is clear that Jay's desire to track down the root cause, a root cause that satisfies his painful struggle with his hurtful history, was not adequately attended to in previous helping attempts. His perception was that no one wanted to take the time to really delve into his problem.

The client not only defined his wants, but has also identified the criterion for success in treatment, namely, finding the cause of his distress. It seemed that the act of identifying a root cause would somehow legitimize or justify his suffering. This provided direct guidance for the team about possible directions. For success to occur, therapy must provide a context for Jay to answer his questions; to discount his request or ignore his desire for insight in favor of a pure focus on solutions, exceptions, or problem interruption would likely fall short, just as previous attempts had. Insight may not be a necessary precondition for change for everyone, but it seemed that, for Jay, it was. Therefore, the team's task was to involve Jay in the process of identifying the root cause; to create the opportunity for the discovery of possible root causes.

The case of Jay illustrates how making treatment fit the expectations and desires of the client is critically important. While no model or method rings true for everyone, it is very difficult to go wrong when giving clients exactly what they ask for. Molding treatment to the client's expectations and desires all but guarantees a positive outcome. The team deliberated and focused their efforts in the context of Jay's theory of change. Rather than discuss the many different interventive strategies, the team devoted itself to providing a possibility-filled process directed by Jay's construction of what constituted success in therapy. The team sought to help Jay determine what was wrong with him.

The following "intervention" was solely for the purpose to enlist Jay's participation in discovering a root cause.

Excerpt Three

T: Hope we didn't keep you long. Therapists are a long-winded group. There are a couple of things we as a team want to convey to you. We really think that you are on to something in terms of wanting to find out what's wrong and the root cause. We agree that finding out what is wrong has been given short shrift. People have given you an easy answer that most people like to hear.

They told you that you are fine, you have a good head on your shoulders, and everything is okay. And they've not been able to give you the kind of feedback that you're looking for so you can determine the root cause and make the changes you need to do. They unfortunately didn't want to mess with you. That's what people have done, they have not wanted to mess with you or to take the time to find out what's really wrong.

We will take the time this situation deserves. But, as far as the root cause goes, we frankly don't know because it could be a lot of different things. Just from our short conversation with you today, the team talked about all the things that have happened to you in your life that could be root causes to some of things you are experiencing now. You started early on in life with some big, traumatic circumstances. The first grade experience, the fifth grade teacher, the failing out of seventh, being a retard. I mean on and on and on—rejections, not getting your father's approval, trouble with women, people not accepting you, people not wanting you or liking you, one negative, rejecting, experience on top of another. So, all that has combined in such a way that you are having these problems, these symptoms, and you are not really sure what the root cause is.

There were some discussions about that, the root cause, and people have some ideas about that, but you know this is not black and white stuff. We would like to take a deliberate approach and give this issue the time and attention it deserves. We'd like to think about things and unfold this a little bit. We can't magically identify it and give you a prescription. I wish that it was that simple, but humans are far more complicated than that. And, as you know, this is a complex situation and we don't want to make any hasty judgments. We want to talk about you and your life and what some of the possibilities of those root causes are. We want to share those possibilities with you, and then we need your input, because some things will ring truer than others and we need your feedback about that. Along with that, we need to learn more about what's wrong now so that we may then tie that to the root cause. So, we wanted to ask you to do something between now and the next time we get together. Is that okay with you?

J: What is it that you want me to do?

T: What we'd like you to do is to note the times that you feel there's something wrong with you, so you can describe those situations to us and give us more input into the ways the root cause gets expressed. From that, we can try to determine the root cause, so that we can figure out what's wrong with you. This may help narrow the field a little bit, because there are so many possible root causes.

Commentary

The client's theory of change is unequivocally stated. He believes that there is something very wrong and he wants to get to the bottom of it. The team honors that theory and validates his view that no one has given him direct feedback or taken enough time to figure it out. The team strongly conveys the desire to see this through and give his problem the time and attention it deserves. The suggestion to gather more information directly validates the client's theory of a root cause and joins him in the discovery process. The suggestion conveys that the team is taking the time to find out what is going on. The suggestion, while focused on what's wrong, depended on the client's analytical skills, directly addressed his desires for therapy, and intended to make Jay a partner in the search for the root cause. The task is congruent with the client's theory because it asks the client to observe the times that exemplify what is wrong with him, essentially the antithesis to a solution- or competency-based intervention.

Observation tasks extend the exploration process to between sessions, hoping to capitalize on client resources and enable clients to discover possibilities that may resolve their dilemmas. These tasks enlist client participation in the exploration and discovery process; they are attempts to empower events in clients' lives between sessions that they may utilize to resolve their problems. Observation tasks, therefore, promote change that occurs from client factors (Miller et al., 1997) and often lead to insight-like experiences (Duncan & Solovey, 1989).

At this point in the consultation, Carrie was on the edge of her seat waiting, and actually hoping, to see the end-of-session emotional storm because she especially wanted ideas to interrupt what she considered an intolerable situation. The consulting therapist battened down the hatches and was ready for the storm. The message to the client regarding taking things slowly and deliberately also applied to the therapist and the team. The team truly realized that regardless of the client's desperation, they needed to lean to the client's theory and counter any impulses to give quick answers.

Excerpt Four

J: I'm finding it increasingly harder to keep opening this emotional scab, to come in for one hour, let the pus come out, then come back in two weeks and we'll do it again. I'm finding it extremely difficult to continue doing that [getting louder, pitch raising].

T: That must be very tough.

J: I can't tolerate it any more. What can I do? I want to do what you want me to do. I want to fully cooperate. This last month has been hell. It is a big emotional problem [standing up, starting to cry]. I can't keep doing this!

T: It really has got to be excruciating for you, because I know we drag all this stuff out, and you experience all this pain and anguish, and then we say, "Well, gotta go Jay, see ya next time." It's tough. It's really tough.

J: [Sobbing, pleading] And one of the things I thought about coming was that it wouldn't do any good. Because I'll sit down for an hour and pour my guts out, then it'll be "see ya next week." Please, can you help me [nearly screaming], I hurt so much!

T: Uh-huh, unfortunately, that's a possibility, that it won't help, but I do guarantee you that we will do our honest best.

J: I'm not getting anything back [still standing and crying].

T: I'm really sorry that the only thing we can give back now is to ask you to get more data for us, and to reassure you we won't pass you on to someone else. We know that's really inadequate, but we are stuck with the complexity of this situation. If there's anything else we can do let me know.

J: I'll do it. I'm not fighting you. I'm just really discouraged.

T: No wonder, you have been struggling with this for a long time. I wish we could do something that would make this process easier, but I don't know what that would be. If there were an easy answer, you wouldn't be here. If we could give an answer in one session, it wouldn't be worth listening to.

J: [Sitting down, voice lowering] If there were short-term solutions or bandages or medication, then there would not be a need for this. It would be easily resolved, like everybody has been telling me.

T: That's right.

J: I can sit and rationalize with you all day, but no one understands the human mind, how it really functions and works.

T: That's so true.

J: We are very complex, not even the computer can ever come close to emulating how the human mind works.

T: You're so right. Jay, I really appreciate your sharing that with us because you're telling me that you understand how difficult this task really is. I appreciate you giving us that validation and also sharing your pain that you wish it would happen more quickly. I can't feel your pain, but I can sure see it and I do certainly appreciate your desire to get it over with. I also really appreciate your understanding that we human beings are very complex creatures and that we need to work with this for a while to try to make some sense out of it.

J: Thanks, you've given me a direction. I realize that I told Carrie it's a lot of pieces to a puzzle; it's a 1000-piece puzzle and she's got to sort it out and put it together and it's not going to be easy for her.

T: You're right, you're right on the money.

J: I told her I was going to be a challenge to her. If I could reduce my problem I wouldn't be sitting here. I cannot intellectually determine what is wrong. I'm missing something here. I can give you the 1000 pieces, but I can't put the puzzle together.

T: Uh-huh, I really appreciate your bearing with us.

Commentary

Jay again displayed his pain, stating that it was so hard to keep opening this wound and to get nothing in return. The therapist stayed in Jay's world, stating that it was very difficult to get so little encouragement, but that the team wanted to take the time to weigh out the options and to make good judgments in this very intricate case. The end-of-session storm was calmed because the client's theory was honored.

The therapist was certainly anxious during this exchange, but felt both confident in the direction taken and supported by the team. The therapist had ample opportunity to take his own pulse in this case, given the team was always handy to remind him to stay focused on the client's goals, regardless of the emotionality of the client.

Despite his desperate pleadings for answers and relief from pain, Jay wanted to know the root cause of what is wrong. He did not want a simple answer or a Pollyannish affirmation of his strengths and resources. The consulting therapist did not give false hope or make any statements that would in any way diminish either what was wrong with him or his experience of pain. Validating Jay's viewpoint, rather than his strengths, enabled him to calm down. Note how he not only calmed down, but reiterated his view that this was a long-term and very complex issue, "a 1000-piece puzzle." Any suggestion to the contrary would risk violating his trust and minimizing his life-long, identity-forming problem. Accepting a quick fix answer of any kind (e.g., overreacting or medication) would represent a significant loss of face for Jay.

The client's response to the team's suggestion and his simple "thanks" indicated a favorable alliance and the team thought they were on the right track. Accommodating Jay's view of the alliance was perhaps best served by honoring Jay's persistence in finding out what was wrong. The alliance was therefore enhanced by reinforcing the complexity of the situation and not providing any quick answers. Because Jay's theory of change could only be honored by confirmation that something was wrong, previous therapies missed the opportunity to accommodate Jay's frame of reference regarding how therapy would best address his needs.

Subsequent actions on the part of previous helpers, therefore, were incongruent with Jay's theory of change. The more incongruous the client's theory and the therapist's approach, the more impossible the pathway. In retrospect, it is easy to identify the pathways to impossibility that converged to transform this case with potential into one with little or no possibility for change.

Inattention to Motivation

Recall that an unproductive and futile therapy can come about by mistaking or overlooking what the client wants to accomplish, misapprehending the client's readiness for change, or pursuing a personal motivation. In the six sessions before the consultation, Jay had stated that he wanted to be "fixed." His statements were usually belabored with tears and pleadings of strong intensity. The referring therapist paid attention to Jay's statements but overlooked Jay's true motivation—to find out "what's wrong with me." Consequently, the therapist focused on how he might solve his problems

Another pathway to impossibility was Jay's need to save face. No one confirmed his view that something was wrong (at least to his satisfaction). He wanted confirmation that there was something wrong, he wanted validation that his struggle had been worth going through, and he wanted the struggle named. The referring therapist's view of change negated his view with affirmations that he had come so far, been so successful, and had significant resources.

While Jay was motivated and ready for action, his perceptions of motivation and change were far different than the therapist's. The more his perceptions were misunderstood, the more frustrated he became. Jay needed to know what was wrong; he needed to examine and analyze his past, and give time, credence, and purpose to his pain. The therapist's personal motivation to move him forward fostered a misconception of his motivation and focused on helping to "fix" him. These factors presented significant roadblocks to positive outcome.

Theory Countertransference

The application of some tenets of solution-oriented therapy also produced roadblocks to change for Jay. As the referring therapist tried to validate Jay's resources, skills, and abilities and search for exceptions and solutions, she was blinded to the possibility that Jay's core identity seemed an integral component of his emotional struggle. How could such an immense amount of pain and suffering be taken lightly, treated quickly, and dismissed as no longer necessary? Jay needed to name his pain, perhaps more than recover from it. This was his pathway to change. Once named, it became valid and purposeful, a reflection of who he had become in the struggle.

In looking for "solutions" to the problem of emotional turmoil, the therapist applied her own theory of treatment. In doing so, she moved in a directly opposite direction from the client, serving only to frustrate him. Hope to the therapist meant building upon resources, healing, and moving forward; to the client, hope meant confirmation that past identity was still valid in the present, that his struggle would not be quickly overlooked, but would be appreciated for the fight it had been and continued to be. Hope meant that others around him would recognize his struggle, not his success.

When the consultation sessions focused on naming the struggle, identifying its cause, and validating its long-term complexity, the client was infused with hope. When hope was present, roadblocks began to fade and the pathways to possibility opened.

Between sessions, the team met, reviewed the tape of the first session, and focused on Jay's theory. The team speculated that Jay needed to know what was wrong so that he could maintain his identity. All of his life he had been rejected and abandoned. He had struggled and in many cases had overcome tremendous odds. From Jay's perspective, his identity was founded in his struggle to overcome. That very struggle gave purpose to his pain. If nothing was wrong with him, or if he could "fix himself," then all of the struggle would become invalid and his identity would be lost. It was far more important to Jay, the driving motivation of his therapy in fact, to find out what was wrong. The team took that motivation seriously. Honoring Jay's theory, the team worked to identify "root causes" of what could be wrong. Three root causes were presented to Jay at the next session.

SESSION TWO

Excerpt One

T: We have talked at some length and viewed the tape. A lot of interesting ideas were presented. But first, we would like to get your feedback on the homework task that we gave you to help us discover the root cause.

J: All right, I did some praying and soul searching. I wrote some notes.

T: Okay. Good.

J: I just want to read this thing off. I'm attempting to express my
     fears and what might be the underlying problem of my behavior.
     I find this method of communication — meaning writing — as be-
     ing helpful to me. I find when I am by myself, I can write
     thoughts down, I can get a really better, more intimate view of
     myself. I broke them down into fears and problems.

T: Okay.

J: Fears. This is an intense fear: I'm afraid that if I tell you what my
     problem is, then for the sake of convenience you will agree with
     it, give me a few words of encouragement and send me on my
     way. My fear is that you will not take time to look deeper and
     help me. I need constant reinforcement that you will fight this
     fight with me. There's been too many discouragements in my
     previous attempts at getting to the bottom of this.

T: Umhm. Everybody just wanted to pat you on the back and get
     rid of you. We won't do that. We will see this through however
     long it takes. We are in this for the duration.

J: I'm afraid if I get angry, people will leave me. One time a counse-
     lor tried to do anger therapy with me. I feel I could not do it
     because I was afraid of rejection if I did get angry. That's one of
     my problems. I do not get angry at people. I'm afraid to be alone,
     I need the security that people care about me. Not being wanted
     and appreciated frightens me. I find myself being drawn to peo-
     ple that acknowledge me, which in itself is not bad, but I want
     more than what they can offer.

T: Okay.

J: My wife, we really can't talk about my problems, she just does not
     seem to understand my feelings. Since there are no physical wounds
     on me, she does not know how to treat me, she does not know
     how to talk to me. She's gotta understand that I'm hurting on the
     inside. But she can't empathize with me. She can't sympathize with
     me, and it's building up a barrier and I'm trying to break it down
     by being honest and trying to express my feelings with her.
         But she is not understanding. She will admit she is not a very
     sympathetic person. For example, I was sick with a cold and she
     thought I was acting and I really wasn't as sick as I was, but then
     she got it two days later and realized I was not faking it.

T: So it sounds like she gives you the same message, that there's nothing wrong with you, you are pretending, and are making a big deal out of something that isn't.

J: Right. When I had leg surgery, she could see the pus coming out of the leg. She was sympathetic to that because it's something tangible she could see. It's this thing in our society that since I can't see anything wrong with you, there must not be anything wrong with you.

T: Right.

J: Problem. I'm not able to communicate what I am feeling which is leading to emotions, anger, and frustrations being held back. I wrote that I feel lost in myself, I cry for help and no one hears my voice. Deep down there is a need not being met and I do not know how to vocalize it. I think this is because as a child, I was forbidden from expressing my feelings of dissatisfaction. If I did not like something my father did, that was too bad. I'm scared. I don't know how to vocalize any dissatisfaction or anger. And it's wrong for me to do that. I'm so scared of being put down all the time. All right, *here's the root cause—I'm insecure.* I can only conclude that I never developed a healthy self-esteem as a child. As a teenager, looking to establish and discover who I am, I got the repeated message from a sibling and a peer group that I was a retard, that there's something wrong with me. That we don't want to hear from you or care about you and do not want you around. Okay, now this is the question I wrote. Does this account for my desires today to be accepted by others no matter what the emotional cost to me?

T: Makes a lot of sense.

J: 'Cause I'm looking for acceptance. Today I find myself at the mercy of others for my self-identity and self-esteem. Okay, my self worth is based on other people's opinion of me. I feel I must reach some standards of perfection. I'm constantly seeking the approval of others. Okay, I know I am not a psychologist, but I feel a lot of hurt and frustration and confusion is resided in my subconscious because of my past experience. I'm thinking my subconscious won't let me express myself for fear that maybe my siblings and friends were right. I feel a rush of emotions coming out now! [Voice intensifying, starting to cry] Maybe I am scared they are right, that maybe I am really a retard and there is something wrong with me.

T: Okay.

J: I think that's it, because when I read this statement, I really feel deep down inside that in my subconscious there is something. It's like a person who can't walk, there's nothing wrong with them physically, but they're so convinced they can't walk, that they can't do it. I feel that is my problem. Consciously, I know there is a problem, but my subconscious just won't let go of it. I don't know if that's a sound theory or doctrine or not. I feel that I am an insecure person. I believe somewhere in my emotional self-identity development years as a child, something went wrong when I was trying to figure out who I am and establish my own identity.

T: That makes a lot of sense.

J: My anger, frustrations, and self-expectations are just manifestations of my insecurity. I just don't have the confidence in many areas of my life because I don't have the internal resources to deal with situation. I resort to my emotions. That's the only way I know how to communicate is through my emotions. I believe what hinders me from getting well is locked up in my subconscious.

T: Okay.

J: Now, I feel like I am this burn patient, though I never suffered severe burns, but the therapy for burns is that you have to unwrap the wrapping, remove that growth of skin to allow for the healing, because the healing has to come from the inside out. I feel like that burn patient. When I come to therapy sessions, whatever healing that has taken place is now just ripped off of me and now I'm just exposed again. It takes several days to get over the trauma from coming to these therapy sessions. My question is, if I have to go through that, then I will. I don't like it and I don't want to go through it anymore, I'm tired of it. This has to stop people; I'm sincere when I say that. It's like the burn patient, if that's the only way to heal, from inside out, then I have no choice, you have to tell me if there's any other way to heal. I tell you I don't like the present way we are doing this.

T: Okay.

J: I want to start dealing with the positive things. I know what I am capable of doing, there's a wealth of power and an infinite amount of potential waiting within. I'm so arrogant and over-confident when I get by myself, then when people are around me, I'm too nervous with them around me. I'm afraid I will make a mistake. I'm scared that if you see me make a mistake that you will ridicule me or maybe make fun of me.

T: Okay, this wealth of power is there when you are alone, but when you are in the presence of another person, the subconscious something that's wrong with you prevents you from being able to express it.

J: Yes, that's my theory. And there's the piece I did for you [hands the therapist a paper].

T: Okay, well it sounds like you did a lot of soul searching and it was very productive. You figured out what is wrong with you!

J: It is my theory of the subconscious. I really feel, when I wrote this, I was really in touch with my subconscious. There were times that I would have to stop and cry because I'm obviously in tune with something. I did this thing and it brought up a lot of emotions. It hit something in the subconscious because tears started to come out.

T: So there was a ringing of truth as you were experiencing it. Great, that's wonderful!

J: I want to shake, I'm scared [crying].

T: Well, it's very frightening to get that close to your core and try to understand it and see what comes out of it. That's great.

J: There is insecurity in all of these thing I'm manifesting. Could they be symptoms of being insecure?

T: Yes, sure they can, especially the way you describe it and what you wrote. Absolutely. And, I'm jumping ahead of myself a little bit, one of the major theories that we were going to present to you today about what we feel is wrong is very close to what you just presented. Three words struck us all as we were looking at this situation: scars, injustices, and rejections—never quite able to get your father's approval, people labeling you and rejecting you, and not fitting in. And you are right, that creates a circumstance of not being able to get the feeling of security from other people. And so your theory is right in line with one of the major ones we were talking about.

J: Why can I diagnose myself to your level and yet not help myself?

T: Well, because identifying and solving a problem are two different things. Again, it's very different to turn that inward to yourself and to find your own solution out of it. It's very difficult and complex, but yes I think your theory is certainly on the mark, especially since you had a strong internal reaction to it. What I would like to do now is to take a break and discuss what you presented today with the team.

J: But the one thing that's going to have to be emphasized again is that it took 40 years to get this far and it may take another 40 years to resolve them.

T: That's right, it may take a lifetime. Definitely. And I don't think it's a matter of cure, it's more a matter of improvement and working on it. So I agree, it's far too complex and it's been here too long to have any magic solution. That's not going to work that way. You know that.

Commentary

Enlisting Jay's participation in discovering the root cause pays off. Jay, through his own devices and efforts, figures out what is wrong with him: He is insecure because of his childhood history of rejections. Note that Jay did not follow the suggestion to the "letter," but rather invented his own application with favorable results. One efficient session of honoring his theory of finding out what is wrong with him, and accommodating his view that he had previously been dismissed by helpers not wanting to mess with him, promotes significant movement. Jay has identified his root cause. He is quick to point out, however, that the problem remains a long-term one and still cannot be dismissed easily.

While the identification of a root cause is dramatic movement in this case, the team still has to be cautious about jumping on the bandwagon of change because any such movement may be perceived as not wanting to mess with the problem. As promised, the team takes a deliberate approach and continues with the presentation of possible root causes.

Excerpt Two

T: We were very impressed by your theory of the subconscious and insecurity, especially given that we spent over an hour discussing it this morning and it fit everything that we were talking about. That was the predominant view; the theory of scars, injustices, and rejections, not being able to please your father, never developing feelings of acceptance or security, and all the traumatic things that occurred in your horrendous childhood.

J: Why do you consider it horrendous?

T: Well, it's pretty horrendous to be told that you are a retard, you don't fit in, and to not have any friends—that's pretty horrendous.

J: Okay.

T: You'll be hard-pressed to talk us out of that you had a traumatic childhood.

J: People have worse, kids are beaten.

T: True, but how do you put a price tag or level of severity on being totally crushed emotionally as a child versus being slapped around as a child? I don't know how to evaluate which is worse on a person's psyche. I know they are both pretty damn bad. How do you quantify suffering?

J: Good point.

T: The theory you presented today is very congruent with the major view that was evolving from the team and we really were genuinely impressed with what you came up with—especially since we came up with it too [laughs].

J: But I still have this fear that you are just agreeing with me, so you won't have to mess with me.

T: We have a couple of other views as well. And because we agree doesn't mean there's not a long rocky road ahead. We're still developing and working with the predominate theory. Whether it is the truth with a capital T, we're not at that level of certainty, but that is the way we are leaning toward. Especially since you came up with it in response to your own efforts, and had the emotional connection while you were doing it. This makes us think it is pretty close, because that's a good measure on how good theories are, they ring true emotionally, and you expressed that quite articulately. But there are a couple of other ideas the team talked about.

One was that, yes, all this stuff makes sense about your childhood and past, but also we can't eliminate the possibility that this is related to a very complicated and unresolved grief process concerning your father's death. One person on the team felt that the closeness in time of when a lot of this started happening with you and your father's death may point to that possibility.

J: You have a point here. There's lots that I will never know, because of his death. So there might be some merit to the person that brought it up.

T: Okay, that was one. Another one is, I don't know if this makes any sense, because of these life experiences, the thing that most affects your behavior and how you present yourself to others and these problems you're having, is that you have the view that something is wrong with you and that dictates your behavior. In other words, the only thing wrong with you is that you think there is something wrong with you.

J: I thought about that too; I may have convinced myself so much that there is something wrong with me that I actually believe it and am going with that premise.

T: Yes, that's exactly it, that was the view expressed very clearly behind the mirror.

J: Maybe there's nothing wrong with me. Maybe I enjoy getting the sympathy off other people, but people can only go so far, and tolerance-wise people don't like to be around people who are always upset.

T: So true.

J: But they certainly will come to your need for a short time, and I get upset when they start pulling away because they can no longer give me that. So I thought about that too and never came to a conclusion.

T: Okay, so there could be some merit to that also, but I guess that just reinforces that this is a very complex set of issues.

J: I knew that coming into here.

Commentary

Note how Jay challenged the statement about his childhood in the same fashion that others have minimized his painful experiences. The team believed that Jay was testing our resolve to see if we were just agreeing with him to patronize him. Therefore, it was not considered a risk to respond to the challenge because the therapist's response directly validated the client's theory of insecurity.

The therapist offered two other theories of possible root causes. Both theories emerged from the client's presentation and validated his view of his situation. Jay acknowledged that he had considered both options but had come to no conclusions about either of them. The therapist reiterated that this was indeed a very complex issue, requiring further deliberation and discussion. The following excerpt concludes the session.

Excerpt Three

T: These are possibilities, and we're leaning toward the predominant view of the insecurity hypothesis, and that's what we would like to give more thought to, how to address this complex situation. The team and you have identified the problem, a possible root cause, and we will like to pursue that, of course, with your permission and help. You brought up a very interesting point earlier about how to pursue this once you've identified it. You made the analogy of the burn patient. That's an excellent analogy. That is one way to approach a problem of the subconscious. There are other ways to approach it as well, that do not require the unwrapping and pulling off the dead skin to heal from within. So just as there are multiple theories of root causes, there are multiple ways of addressing those root causes. And that is what we would like to give some consideration to, to think about ways to address the insecurity, this unconscious block, so that you can address the problem of being able to be confident with others the way you are with yourself, and apply the advice you give to others to yourself. Jay, does this make sense as a way to go for us at this point?

J: Well, you haven't given me a way to go. You just said we have three hypotheses, one we feel is the predominant, one we would like to explore in more detail, the one of insecurity that I also experienced as true. You haven't given me a plan of how you're going to do that.

T: You're right. There are a lot of different ways, a lot of different plans. So, again, we want to think about the ways to do it, but I'm wondering if the direction of pursuing the insecurity theory is the way you want to go, does it seem reasonable to you?

J: What should I do?

T: We wanted to ask you to do another task for us, more specific to the insecurity theory. When you are with other people and you observe yourself not being confident and feeling like you're going to make a mistake, we would like for you to observe those situations and particularly look at what's going on inside of you, so we can get more info about your subconscious. This is kind of an outside-in way of approaching it rather than an inside-out. But it may be that it requires inside-out addressing, we don't know.

J: I have tried consciously when I walk into a situation, how am I communicating to other people — not verbally, I mean in a non-verbal — am I giving them clues, am I losing the eye contact.

T: This is a little bit different, those are more conscious things you are doing. What we are suggesting is when you are in the throes of a situation, a situation in which you feel those familiar pains of insecurity, usually the time when you are not paying attention to what's happening inside you, we would like for you to get intentionally more internally focused in terms of what's preventing you from being confident. We will think of ways to pursue it, both outside-in and inside-out, to discuss with you next time after hearing what you discover. So that's where we'd like to go, if that seems to make sense to you.

J: Okay, yes it does, right. I have never tried to understand what is happening inside me during those times. I'm usually focused on how I'm coming across and what the other person is doing.

T: And if you could, please, as you did this time, write it out because that seemed to provide a direct conduit to your inner experience, your subconscious.

J: Okay, I'll continue my self-diagnosis on the PC, just allowing my emotions to come out. I know that this is no 3- or 4-session dilemma.

T: That's for sure!

Commentary

The therapist drew on an analogy that the client had used earlier, referring to him as a "burn patient." The therapist connected that analogy to dealing with the subconscious, careful to validate Jay's view of things, but also to suggest that there were other ways to approach the insecurity problem as well. The team gave Jay an assignment meant to help him begin to get to the block in his subconscious. Jay agreed to focus on his internal response to situations that were examples of what was wrong. The client restated his view that the process would likely take a long time. He did not want therapy that lasted only three or four sessions. The therapist agreed.

Given the positive movement from the previous session, the team decided to continue on the same course. The "intervention" arose from the client's presentation, validated his theory of change, and encouraged his further self-diagnosis. The intervention was essentially invented, formulated from the client's theory, and designed specifically for his circumstances. Further, it continued to validate his view of what was wrong as well as what had already worked in the treatment process. It depended on his abilities and enlisted his participation. Note how in this session there was no end-of-session outpour of emotion—the first time in eight sessions. The team believed they were onto something! An appointment was scheduled for two weeks.

Follow-Up

Early the next week, Jay's referring therapist received a call from Jay. He explained that there were many things taking place at his work and with his family, and he felt that he could not devote himself to dealing with his problems at this point. The insecurity problem still existed, but it was better. Other things were more important: a huge corporate buyout, job changes, boss changes, and illness of his children presented new struggles for Jay—current ones—which allowed him to set aside the old struggle, and in his own way, move forward.

Carrie remained in Jay's frame of reference, asking if he would be able to handle the tremendous emotional upheaval already present, now with the added stress from other areas. Jay said that he was feeling more confident and that he could handle things on his own. The therapist suggested that since it was a long-term process, he could come back to it when things settled down; the team would be very willing to continue to work with him.

Jay returned one year later for one session. In that session, he stated that he had no further problems with his insecurity, but had felt slightly depressed recently. His physician had just diagnosed him with hypothyroidism for which he was taking medication. Jay decided in session that he would take the medication for a while to see if it regulated his depressive symptoms, but would come back if he was having difficulty. There was no emotional storm at the end of the session. Jay did not return.

DISCUSSION

Jay exemplifies the pathways to impossibility and the efficient treatment of psychotherapy veterans. Inattention to the client's motivation to determine the root cause of his distress, combined with a relentless therapeutic pursuit of solutions (theory countertransference), resulted in an escalating spiral of frustration in both the client and therapist. Jay also illustrates the importance of the client's participation in the treatment process. In this case, it is really more accurate to say that once therapy became collaborative and participated with Jay in searching for a root cause, it became efficient and encouraged Jay to discover his own way out of his dilemma. Although Jay stated that his struggle would take a lifetime in therapy, he identified it in one session and overcame it in two. The referring therapist summarizes this case as follows:

The intensity of Jay zapped me every time I worked with him. As I look back over my notes, I realize that what I tried to see as progress for Jay was what frightened him most. He was certainly a motivated client, but his motivation was far different than mine. I do not believe that Jay was offended by the work we did together. I believe perhaps this was his only experience at "saving face" in a counseling setting. Yet, to some degree I may have violated his identity by not really hearing his motivation for treatment. I realize that I got stuck in the content and missed the motivation, and applied what I still consider to be great theory in a situation where it did not match this client's frame of reference. This is hard work. It's no wonder therapists decide these cases are impossible.

It is interesting to note that Jay believed he could now handle things on his own — just as many had told him — but only realized after his expedition for the root cause had been legitimized and his struggle validated. Jay's return for a session with Carrie indicated his satisfaction with her as a therapist and reinforced the team's view that Jay had finally obtained what he needed from therapy.

The client's heightened emotionality, which had been seen as a sign of borderline pathology, virtually vanished when he was taken seriously. Limits did not have to be set or controls imposed. What worked best was validation of his desires to identify what was wrong with him. In service of supporting his quest for the root cause (and thereby forging a strong alliance), an effort was made to encourage insight — a goal deemed important in the psychodynamic tradition. In this instance though, the insight was not offered through the technique of interpretation; instead, the client discovered insight through his own efforts that enabled him to get on with his life.

EPILOGUE

when serpents bargain for the right to squirm
and the sun strikes to gain a living wage —
when thorns regard their roses with alarm
and rainbows are insured against old age

when every thrush may sing no new moon in
if all screech-owls have not okayed his voice
— and any wave signs on the dotted line
or else an ocean is compelled to close

when the oak begs permission of the birch
to make an acorn — valleys accuse their
mountains of having altitude — and march
denounces april as a saboteur

then we'll believe in that incredible
unanimal mankind(and not until)

E. E. Cummings

CHAPTER 9

Impracticability: Taking a Different Path

We do no great things; only small things with great love.

Mother Theresa

THIS CHAPTER RECOUNTS the principal points of the book by presenting the case that taught us the most about impossibility. This case piqued our curiosity and started our quest for answers; we were humbled by this case. It highlights the pitfalls of assuming an expert, noncollaborative position. It also shows the surprising resilience of individuals freed from the constraints of impossibility. Once the therapy avoids the pathways of impossibility and accommodates the clients' resources and frame of reference, a floundering treatment is salvaged.

In addition, the implications of considering the client's frame of reference as the knowledge base of psychotherapy is summarized. In this context, an evaluation of the advantages and disadvantages of theory and client-directed approaches to human problems is provided.

THE CASE OF EILEEN AND RICHARD

Eileen spent one year in a psychiatric unit specializing in chemical dependency and personality disorders. After discharge, she attended four sessions of psychotherapy per week for a year. Because the treatment facility was approximately 100 miles from her home, the client stayed in an apartment, away from her husband, Richard.

Eileen and Richard had been separated for close to two years. They came requesting marital therapy to help them adjust to their reunification. The resumed relationship had been fraught with difficulties, including an escalating pattern of violence, self-mutilation, and suicide attempts.

SESSION ONE

Excerpt One

T: What brings you here to see me today?

R: We've actually been in therapy together for over two years now. Well, just to give you a little background, we were married in '83, we had dated for a year. We had a very good courtship, as far as our being able to communicate with each other. Within about six months of the time we got married, she began to show symptoms of stress and inability to cope. It first appeared with work: inability to get to work on time and feeling very stressed out by her job and the pressure of the corporate world. Things started deteriorating and the effects started to show on our relationship. Things progressively got worse until, after a couple violent outbursts, we decided to get some help. At that time it was identified that alcohol might be a problem, and she was hospitalized for five weeks, and then went back to work for a couple months, and then was hospitalized again and started taking lithium. Bipolar depression was the diagnosis. Things still did not get any better. She was not working, and we decided to try another route, and we went to a special inpatient program for alcoholics and personality disorders. She continued to be there—both as inpatient and later as outpatient—for over two years. And she's just two or three weeks ago moved back. She was maintaining an apartment near the hospital so she could be in outpatient therapy. So, she was inpatient for a year, then in outpatient six times a week, four individual and two group, until recently. And she still goes back twice a week.

T: You go back twice a week?

E: I go back for group therapy on Monday and Friday night. And I go back Monday afternoon and Thursday afternoon for appointments with Dr. A for individual. The outpatient was more extensive and full time in the beginning and has tapered down for the first time right now.

R: We had, the entire time, family counseling, although the therapist there admits that her function was more toward me than Eileen. I would meet with her every week for maybe half an hour, hour, then we would get together for an hour or so. That continued probably about a year and a half.

T: So you were seeing—I'm sorry, I'm confused by—this is a lot of therapy—[laughs].

E: Yes [laughing], and we're looking for more. And we just terminated with her, the family counselor, two weeks ago.

R: I was also attending a weekly family group therapy. It was a format for families to be involved with patients who were in a compulsive disorders program individually. I'm not resistant at all, but I have gotten burned out.

T: No wonder!

E: It was an intense feeling of burnout. He had feelings of exhaustion.

R: I was putting an average of 15,000 miles a year just driving back and forth to the hospital those two years.

T: My gosh!

E: Okay—I decided to let Rich speak first, because we both came to the conclusion that I am the more verbal one, and I'm definitely the more flamboyant one—and that's gotten me a lot of attention. My perspective is that we've had a lot of involvement with my illnesses and weaknesses and defects. We now find ourselves trying to live together as man and wife. I thought things could be Camelot, and still want it to be. I filter them so heavily the way that only I can—that I have a hard time seeing things as other people do or I just am one very egocentric person. And that's where I am—I don't know how to change that yet, I'm trying to work on changing it. But, I don't really know what it is to be giving. I don't feel like I have a lot to give, I'd like to give what I have, but I don't know how to do that. I don't know how to separate when I hear something. He may say something and says I don't mean it the way you're hearing it—but I'm hearing it that way! Things are worse than I would like to believe them. I don't mean to magnify them any, but I really want to be realistic. I want to face things directly, so that we can both be as content as possible and feel like our home and our relationship is a place where we can draw energy from, and be comfortable with, and be nurtured, rather than a place that we don't understand and is scary, and in need of so much protection, that we can't be open with each other and enjoying each other. With the trauma that we've both been through, I just don't know anymore—we're shell-shocked—like I've been walking through a mine field. And it feels like there may be more ahead that I don't realize. I don't want to subject anybody, nor myself, to more therapy—we've had more therapy . . .

R: It's been rediagnosed, too, from bipolar depression to borderline personality disorder with compulsive overtones, I guess you would call them.

E: For one thing, what I am glad about having this opportunity to be treated like a person in a relationship, rather than a patient. I am glad to be away from the hospital environment where I am always the patient, because I feel like I'm always the problem most of the time anyway. But, this is an opportunity to come in here as two individuals, married to each other, and wanting a relationship with each other that is real viable and healthy. And to get away from always talking, always centering on me. I am an attention getter, I mean I will grab attention. But, I don't wish to do that. I would like to have it be a joint sort of thing, and work on where we are now and where we'd like to go. Does that make any sense?

T: It makes a lot of sense to me and I'm glad to hear you say that. This is an opportunity to put the patient role behind you and focus on making the relationship better now and in the future. I will treat you as a person, not as the diagnosis. I'll leave that for your individual therapy to address.

Commentary

Although the therapist says to Eileen that he will treat her as a person—a statement of his intention to work in partnership on her goal to improve the marriage—that is not what happens. As it turns out, the therapist joins the list of therapists who placed themselves in an expert role. Like those before him, he will wage war on Eileen's symptoms. In so doing, he falls into the trap of "doing more of the same," a slippery slope for impossibility.

The recruitment to doing more of the same came from an unexpected place, the therapist's theory countertransference. Looking back, he realized that, in part, he accepted this case to prove that his way of working (at the time, brief strategic therapy) would succeed where this woman's psychoanalytically-informed treatment had not. The referral for marital work had originated with Eileen's individual provider. He set up the case as a challenge because of his disdain for a strategic approach. The new therapist would show him how misguided the client's therapies to date had been. This was a situation ripe for impossibility.

As seen in the next excerpt, the therapist will find much in need of his ministrations and directives.

Excerpt Two (with Husband)

R: But she's very suicidal, at least it's becoming more and more that way. That's what I'm really afraid of right now. She got in the hospital—she didn't even know there were compulsions like bulimia and anorexia. But especially bulimia—she developed that in the hospital. She developed compulsive shopping. Now, it's cutting on herself. She'll get mad—and I don't know if it's for attention or what—she'll take the knife and cut slashes on her arms and legs. Well, the one therapist told me, she's been there twenty years, she said it was one of the worst cases they've ever had. She was in a year of denial in the hospital before she'd admit she was an alcoholic. And she'd, she kept using me as her therapist, and she still does this—rather than use her primary therapist. And they would deny her seeing me for even weeks. And now that we're living together I enable her in some ways. That's my nature, to enable. I help people. That's basic. I do all the cooking, I've done all the laundry, you know, everything. That was before even she got sick. Some people told me they never thought she'd get this far, because of the seriousness of her compulsion and the ramifications of this borderline personality disorder.

But she's so insecure. There's such anger at times. It just comes out. And since she's been home a couple times she's come after me with a knife. A week or so ago, I heard her sharpening the knife. I said, "What are you doing?" She said, "If I'm gonna do it I'm gonna do it right." Then she got— and I went over and tried to take the knife away, and she came after my ankles. She got thrown to the floor. Whether or not she was actually gonna do it or not I don't know. It's a point where I dread to come home at night.

T: I don't blame you. It sounds terrible. What problem concerns you the most in your marriage, or in her right now?

R: I guess the biggest fear is that things will never be any better. And quite honestly, I feel that things have deteriorated since she came home. I guess I just have a fear that things will continue to deteriorate. I keep telling myself that it's just a transitional period. And maybe it is. I don't know. Dr. A is not a person who tells you what's going on. I realize he doesn't want to betray her confidence. But he's seen her literally more than I have for the past two years. It's hard for me to really know where we are at. I have no idea of how he feels or how they interpret all this.

T: So your biggest fear is things will never get better. What's you biggest concern with her, or with your marriage?

R: I'm afraid personally about her, that she'll commit suicide, at some point, accidentally or on purpose.

Commentary

Over the next six sessions, propelled by his anxiety and zeal to prove the invariable power of his approach, the therapist heroically intervened. He cleverly reframed the fights and Eileen's suicidal threats in a variety of ways, made several suggestions, and delivered prescriptions individually and conjointly. The therapist taught communication skills and mediated discussions of the couple's problems. When that failed, he tried discussing dangers of change and employed other resistance-oriented interventions to jump start the couple into sanity.

In the midst of his attempts to restore the couple's wits, the therapist started losing his own. He felt stuck, alarmed, and impotent. He could not see that with all his "overdoing it" he was doing more of the same. In each session, he thought he was trying a different, if not innovative approach. Yet, at a meta-level his tactics were just variations on the theme of "therapizing," doing a treatment *on* Eileen and her husband. The couple had already been on the receiving end of a professional campaign for the previous two years. Meanwhile, the violence, self-mutilation, and suicidal behavior continued. Understandably, the primary therapist was considering rehospitalization and was in daily contact with Eileen.

After six turns on the intervention roller coaster, the therapist finally admitted his approach to therapy was not working. He consulted with a team of colleagues. As a result of thinking through his actions with a calm and impartial audience, he decided to be up front with the couple. He would tell them that he did not know what to do next and that he was worried because the couple's situation had only deteriorated since seeing him.

In session seven, the therapist presented the outcome of the team discussion and shared his heart-felt concern and apprehension regarding the escalating violence. He said he thought he had become, and that therapy in general had become a part of, if not *the* problem. This admission was genuine; it was not intended as strategic leveraging or legerdemain.

The team regarded this turn around as more congruent or compatible with the couple's initial presentation. Eileen initially indicated she did not want to be a patient and both had expressed their experience of being burned out on therapy. The therapist hoped that by standing down from his interventional frenzy, the couple might take a more active role in making their lives better. He resolved he would do no more to change these people. He also committed himself to truly treat Eileen as he had promised in the first session. Awaiting the next session, the therapist had no idea what might develop. He only knew the active, noncollaborative, and expert stance he had previously taken with the couple was contributing to their regression.

SESSION EIGHT

Excerpt One

T: How have things been going?

E: Okay. You know, nothing has been too complicated. Considering our recent trend, that's pretty positive. We've had no violent arguments and I haven't cut myself in the past two weeks.

T: That's fantastic. I must admit I am relieved. How do you account for the change?

R: Well I think we were both pretty shaken by what you said to us last time, that you and your team didn't know what else to tell us. I mean, you are the relationship experts. We were stunned to say the least. We talked a lot about that and decided to take more control of our lives. Eileen decided to drop out of group therapy.

E: It is real scary, but we agreed that therapy has become a problem. We have to get our lives together.

Commentary

To the therapist's surprise, the couple made a major change between sessions. Hearing loudly that the therapist was stumped, that the "relationship experts" were befuddled, the couple decided to shoulder responsibility and self-control. Apparently, through the act of firing himself as the interventionist, the therapist accommodated the couple's expressed wish to be rid of therapy. In effect, he created space or room for the couple to become their own relationship experts.

The therapist continues to monitor developments in the next sessions. He refuses, too, any temptation to offer unwanted interventions or tasks. Consequently, an entirely different process was allowed to transpire. Without the pressure to intervene, the therapist becomes free to listen for a change (Miller et al., 1997).

SESSION NINE

Excerpt One

T: How is it going?

E: Simple and good. Five weeks of no violence or harming myself.

T: Great! Some things have changed between you two. I'm not really for sure what that is. Some of the original concerns regarding the violence between you two seems to have somehow changed.

R: Maybe we just got worn out, I don't know. I see a real conscious change where you [Eileen] try to think things through about why you're feeling a certain way, rather than act them out. You're holding back to analyze it and by the time you've analyzed it, you still may be depressed or upset, but your focus is a lot different than it used to be. What do you think?

E: Yeah, I feel that I'm in a lot more control. For example, I was late and I was furious. I was able to say that I was just actually furious at me and furious that I was late, furious that I was feeling this way, furious for whatever. In the past it would have just stopped at that, it would have passed through my gut and probably would have come out a lot more directed at you and probably verbally blaming you. I was able to realize this kind of situation just makes me pay because I look like a ranting lunatic. I realized I was really paying a lot for my actions. I suppose that's different.

R: That's a perfect example of what I was just talking about.

E: So that helps you some to have me recognize my anger is hurting me. I guess I'm tired of being the crazy one.

R: It helps a lot. That's one big difference. I think that's a significant difference from where we were going.

E: There's a completely different way of viewing and feeling going on right now.

R: Another thing, I sometimes protect you from stress and I also protect myself because I know when you get upset that I have a tendency to get upset. So I don't deny that sometimes I do those things and it's not all pure motives. I think I do it for you, but I also do it for myself.

E: It's nice to be aware of that, I appreciate that you admit it. That's different too. Rich is admitting things. I don't feel that I'm the wacko one all the time.

R: And I've come to the conclusion that I'm not a burnout any more, I'm just a brownout. There's a difference.

E: Oh, let's party [all laugh]. We'll bring out a bottle of champagne and you guys can have a glass [all laugh]. Sounds great. That sounds more positive, that's more positive than blackout, isn't it?

T: Yeah, a lot more. We need to wind down. What would you like to do? I think you two are bringing out the healthier aspects of one another in a lot of different ways and have come to important realizations, as well as handling conflict without violence.

E: Things are much better and I have improved. Let's set an appointment for four weeks.

Commentary

As evidenced in this excerpt, the couple continues to act as their own therapists. They speak to each other, instead of directing their comments to the therapist. The therapist simply comments on the productive, egalitarian, and supportive exchanges between Eileen and Richard and stays out of the way. As the two affirm each other and flex their own competency, their self-attributions change. Eileen is beginning to abrogate a patient identity and Richard no longer sees himself as a "burnout." The therapist witnesses, in amazement, the unfolding of new meanings and directions.

Experiencing a sense of self-efficacy and presumably confident that commerce with Richard will stay on a healthier course, Eileen suggests a month-long hiatus from the couples counseling. The therapist agrees.

SESSION TEN

Excerpt One

T: How do you think things are going?

R: No major blow-ups or anything. I think pretty good other than the long-term stresses that both of us have and things that can't be solved by a pill or therapy or anything like that.

E: About the same. Still doing better. I used to not be able to separate things at all when I was stressed out, and now, although there have been times, I am doing better and I am quicker to realize that I am venting and that it's affecting you [Richard]. And that you seem to be less reactive and critical compared to a phase that we have been in before. I think we are doing a lot more just feeling and touching and just being together and just trying to let go of the pain that comes with the inability to control the major stresses that we have individually. I really appreciate that a lot.

R: I think that's an honest appraisal, an accurate appraisal.

T: Things are going better and they haven't escalated for some time now. Three sessions ago my concern was that things were getting worse. Somehow that pattern got turned around and you two have come to some negotiated terms over what needs to happen to prevent that from occurring and improve your relationship. You have taken more control over your lives. Eileen, you are recognizing your anger and how it has hurt you by fingering you as a lunatic. You are handling your anger much better and Rich is admitting his side as well. Things are going pretty well here and there are some changes being made and it occurred to me that maybe I should not get in the way.

What got me and my colleagues struggling was thinking about what the focus would be. What could I possibly suggest better than how you're dealing with things differently on your own? And we kept kind of running into a brick wall and there's a message there. I am interpreting that to meaning that things are rolling along and improving, things are being done at home and in real life that are working and that probably ought to happen, and I probably ought to get out of it. So I am opening this up for discussion. I am proposing that you stop therapy here and allow things to go on knowing you can come back any time, or you can set one for six weeks from now. Now, I also was thinking, that you were reducing your therapy elsewhere, and that means that a lot of these supports are being pulled out, so it would kind of be removing a piece of that as well. So what are you thinking?

Commentary

The therapist clarifies his role and, because Eileen and Richard are doing better with less therapy, he introduces the idea of calling these visits to an end. While one could argue that there is risk in taking this step, particularly in light of Eileen's self-destructive history, the benefits of termination look to be outweighing whatever gains remain from staying in treatment. Based on their self-reports and in-session conduct toward each other, the couple is showing they are ready to graduate from therapy. This is an important development and should be encouraged. Research shows that clients who attribute success to internal causes (increased mastery, control, insight, changes in coping skills and problem-solving) are more likely to experience good long-term results (Weinberger, 1995). By suggesting an end, the therapist supports the clients' assumption of self-responsibility and competence.

Excerpt Two

R: Well, we're all on the same track, in the sense that we did discuss before we came in here what we thought our focus ought to be, and we had a hard time coming up with anything definite in our minds, right? We talked about cutting back, in fact, while you were out of the room; she said I think we ought to cut back.

E: I am scratching my head going I don't really know how or where to focus. Just inventing a focus would feel mechanical, and might indeed just cause discontent. Then nothing for the sake of something should be our focus. We need to continue in a growthful, health-increasing vein like we are. I know that I have a tremendous amount of growing and stabilization to do. Therefore, if we are both able to own our own selves, work on ourselves, get healthier, and less stressed out individually, then our relationship naturally would follow that. In the meantime, if we are able to come together as we have at moments, to work through some of the tougher times that we are involved in, and come together with that sense of unity and purpose, then things will continue to improve. Therefore, in terms of our purpose here, I don't really have one. I like the idea of having the accessibility of coming back prn, or I really like the idea of setting an appointment, although it can be changed somewhere in the future, knowing if we hit rough water, and I feel that this has been a good place for us to meet. Somehow, even if it's hard to decide what exactly has occurred here, it has helped us reestablish control of our lives.

R: I think she is having the same feelings that both of us have had, and yet there's a reluctance there to totally disband right now and that's fine with me, and maybe as we lengthen out the period and things go well, the confidence of that longer period itself will take care of the need.

T: Good point. I think you're right, you have taken control of lives, not therapists or therapy.

Commentary

The couple voice their agreement with the therapist's opinion. Eileen expresses her wish to continue their gains to date, accomplishments that can be maintained without ongoing therapy. She naturally mentions some anxiety about discontinuing completely, but as visits will be available on an as-needed basis, she is assuaged.

The conversation transpiring illustrates both an ending of the old and the beginning of the new. Eileen and Richard are envisioning a life on their own, one that will succeed as a result of what they do. In this last excerpt they look forward to what needs to happen, the adjustments to be made.

Excerpt Three

E: But I know in my heart of hearts that I thought I was marrying somebody to take care of me, you know — hook, line, and sinker. I wanted someone to completely take care of me, I needed taking care of — I wasn't doing a good job myself. I didn't know how poorly I was taking care of myself, how incapable I was, and how I was relying on a substance to just hold me together, but yet there was the danger of dependency on somebody else. I think it's safe to say you [Richard] are a caretaking type person and somehow, in the beginning of the relationship, unconsciously/consciously, we got together. And as we both know intellectually, it doesn't work out and emotionally we've experienced the pain of it not working it out. The danger is for us to lull into some kind of agreement unconsciously, that limits us both, that just keeps us somewhat in a rut, comfortable, not healthy. I hope that you're able to take care of yourself increasingly more than others because you have a lot of people in your life who "solicit being" taken care of. And still you are able to be that special person that you are, that gives so much. Does that make sense to you or is that too many words?

R: Well, one thing that has probably been evident to you, is I think I have withdrawn some of that caretaking within the last month or two. I don't feel the need or responsibility or feel guilty about fixing you food every night.

E: I know, it's great! You went from feel like you had to, to refusing to, to whenever you feel like it.

R: I mean it's still a struggle for me in a sense because I see you weirded-out because you haven't eaten anything, and waiting for me to fix you something, and I don't do it. And those are the times, nine times out of ten, those are the times that we've come closest to getting into it. But we dealt with it.

E: Now that I have less, less therapy commitments, I just really want to get our home in a more stable place. Since less energy is having to be spent battling each other and being hysterical, I just want to spend that energy nurturing our home and us, so that it is less of a chaotic place and so that some of the things that haven't been done for six years or so start to get done.

Commentary

The couple returned for two more sessions, spanning 12 weeks. No further episodes of violence, self-mutilation, or suicide attempts occurred. Eileen and her individual therapist decided, too, that it was time to take a break from treatment.

All four pathways to impossibility were traveled in this case: the anxious anticipation of impossibility, theory countertransference, doing more of the same, and inattention to motivation. When therapy was curtailed and the expert advice/interventions suspended, Eileen and Richard were allowed the room to solve their problems. They had been therapized "every-which-way-but-up" by individual therapy, group therapy, and finally by marital therapy. Numerous rationales and explanations were offered, many suggestions made, and tasks assigned—yet to no avail. It was not the clients' fault; it was the approach. No treatment was the treatment of choice.

DISCUSSION

This early case turned out to be a watershed event. The marital therapist eagerly took the challenge offered by Eileen's individual therapist; he relished the idea of taking the referring therapist out behind the woodshed for a lesson that he would not soon forget. Instead, Eileen and Richard taught the lesson we have never, thankfully, forgotten.

Previously steeped in the mystique around the work of Erickson, Haley, and the entire strategic tradition, we saw ourselves as change agents par excellence. With the right reframe, paradox, technique, or positioning, the problem would yield. We knew the therapeutic relationship mattered, but principally in the sense of creating the right rapport for compliance. And so, out of our expert, almost imperious attitude toward problems, we succumbed to hubris and at times transformed clients into adversaries—especially veterans, or as we called them in those days, "therapist killers." In the starkest terms, they became bothersome carriers of the problem to be solved.

Eileen and her husband rubbed our noses in the limitations inherent to theory, technique, and an expert therapeutic posture. Their seemingly miraculous turnabout forced a recognition of clients' innate strengths and the contribution of a real collaboration. We learned to depend on our clients and place their ideas and participation above our treasured theories and strategies (Duncan, Parks, & Rusk, 1990). We were no longer enamored of theory and technique, but instead found ourselves entranced by the accomplishments of our clients (Duncan & Solovey, 1989). Thereafter, we sought to empower a process that unfolds client competence and encourages client rightful ownership of change.

The case of Eileen and Richard also helped redirect us from a narrow immersion in the writings of family therapy and brief therapy to a serious attention to the research literature, particularly bearing on psychotherapy outcome. Here, the importance of depending on clients' resources and the significance of the therapeutic alliance was realized—the alliance as a major force for change, not some mere means to an end (Duncan, 1992a, 1992b).

The work of Carl Rogers was also rediscovered. The role of empathy, warmth, genuineness, understanding, and mutual affirmation, especially in the client's experience, was understood (Patterson, 1984; Rogers, 1957). Research shows that to clients these are core variables that matter in their improvement, not theories and flashy technique (Duncan et al., 1992). We began to view technique as providing something akin to a magnifying glass: it brings together, focuses, and concentrates the forces of change, narrows them to a point in place and time, and helps them to ignite into action.

Examining the limits of our methods, and for that matter, the limits of all theory-determined approaches, we reevaluated our work and found ourselves letting go of many traditions. Our confidence in shedding layers of psychotherapy convention was bolstered by our findings that with many cases deemed difficult, if not impossible (e.g., borderline, DID, psychotic delusions), there exists no empirically established guidelines for treatment. Although a consensus has developed among clinicians for treating some conditions, consensus is not the same as truth. What is more, as illustrated by the cases in this book, consensus often fails.

Furthermore, even if a research-established "treatment of choice" is said to exist, upon closer empirical scrutiny it is often exposed as largely a myth. Differences between touted "preferred treatments" and other approaches fade when the theoretical orientation of the investigators, the so-called "allegiance effect" (Jacobson & Addis, 1993), is considered. In addition, when dropouts are included, studies of treatments boasting 75% effectiveness rapidly fall to a 50% success rate (see Miller et al., 1997, for a complete discussion).

From our discovery that all approaches are equivalent with respect to outcome, that technique is pale in comparison to the power of client and relationship factors, and that "treatments of choice" refer mainly to the researcher's preferences, we came to see impossibility as partly an epiphenomenon: an unwelcome result of leaving clients out of the process or diminishing the import of their participation. This prompted us to consider our clients' frame of reference, their world view, as the determining "theory" for our work.

LAST CALL FOR THE CLIENT

In considering the advantages and disadvantages of a client- versus theory-directed approach to therapy, we are attempting to be balanced, fair, and end any hostility. This has been and remains difficult. Still incited by the missionary fire of early Ericksonian and strategic therapists, we are comfortable with disparaging other theoretical premises, particularly those that place pathology firmly on the shoulders of the client and promote the therapist as the centerpiece of the process of change. However, now with a better understanding of the research literature and what matters to clients, we see that our "enlightened" frames are often as narrow as the ones we castigated and vilified.

The position we have come to is that there is value in *all* theoretical systems and techniques. Their worth resides not in their claims to truth, but whether a given theory or technique is of help to the client. For instance, if a client is convinced that some variant of psychodynamic understanding is pivotal for change, as it was in Jay's case, then we will honor that belief, consult our insight-oriented resources, and endeavor our best to accommodate it in the therapy. Indeed, we had to learn to trust clients more (than our own opinions) to follow a helpful premise. This is not always easy.

We recognize, too, that clients will always work on their goals. Always. In this respect, clients, regardless of how "disturbed" or impossible they seem, are very conservative. They will stick to their guns and hold fast against pressure to yield what they regard as important or central to their world. Alice and Natalie are cases in point.

And so, any success we have had to date in facilitating a liberation from impossibility has come from placing clients first. We have learned to listen more, turn off the intervention spigot, stay still, and direct our attention to them—recalling, as Ram Dass once said, "The quieter you become the more you can hear." The greater success we have experienced in doing this, the more room clients have had to be themselves, use their own resources, discover possibilities, attribute self-enhancing meanings to their actions, and take responsibility.

We have thoroughly enjoyed being freed from the constraints of "needing to know the right way to practice." Instead, we trust clients to direct therapy because of our faith in their innate wisdom and strength to overcome pain and adversity. Freedom from the pressures of theoretical allegiance has enabled us to listen with care to honor the client's theory of change, as well as avoid the pathways to impossibility.

Reliance on the client and emancipation from model devotion empowers the efficient treatment of psychotherapy veterns. This is not to suggest that this attitude toward clinical work will prove superior to any other. And yet, it holds promise to refuse the pernicious recruitment of impossibility and defeat it once it is in place.

REFERENCES

Aldrich, C. K. (1968). Brief psychotherapy: A reappraisal of some theoretical assumptions. *The American Journal of Psychiatry, 125*, 585–592.

Alexander, L. B., & Luborsky, L. (1986). The Penn helping alliance scales. In L. S. Greenberg & W. M. Pinsof (Eds.), *The psychotherapeutic process: A research handbook* (pp. 325–366). New York: Guilford.

American Psychiatric Association. (1980). *Diagnostic and statistical manual of mental disorders* (3rd ed.). Washington, DC: Author.

American Psychiatric Association. (1987). *Diagnostic and statistical manual of mental disorders* (rev. 3rd ed.). Washington, DC: Author.

American Psychiatric Association. (1994). *Diagnostic and statistical manual of mental disorders* (4th ed.). Washington, DC: Author.

Arkowitz, H. (1992). A common factors therapy for depression. In J. C. Norcross & M. R. Goldfried (Eds.), *Handbook of psychotherapy integration* (pp. 402–432). New York: Basic.

Bachelor, A. (1988). How clients perceive therapist empathy. *Psychotherapy, 25*, 227–240.

Bachelor, A. (1991). Comparison and relationship to outcome of diverse dimensions of the helping alliance as seen by client and therapist. *Psychotherapy, 28*, 534–549.

Beitman, B. D., Hall, M. J., & Woodward, B. (1992). Integrating pharmacotherapy and psychotherapy. In J. C. Norcross & M. R. Goldfried (Eds.), *Handbook of psychotherapy integration* (pp. 533–560). New York: Basic.

Berg, I. K., & Miller, S. D. (1992). *Working with the problem drinker: A solution-focused approach.* New York: Norton.

Bergin, A. E., & Lambert, M. J. (1978). The evaluation of therapeutic outcomes. In S. L. Garfield & A. E. Bergin (Eds.), *Handbook of psychotherapy and behavior change* (2nd ed., pp. 139–190). New York: Wiley.

Beutler, L. E., & Clarkin, J. F. (1990). *Systematic treatment selection: Toward targeted therapeutic interventions.* New York: Brunner/Mazel.

Bohart, A., & Tallman, K. (1996). The active client: Therapy as self-help. *Journal of Humanistic Psychology, 36*, 7–30.

Brinkley, J. R. (1993). Pharmacotherapy of borderline states. *Psychiatric Clinics of North America, 16*, 853–884.

Budman, S. H., & Gurman, A. S. (1988). *Theory and practice of brief therapy.* New York: Guilford.

Butler, S. F., & Strupp, H. H. (1986). Specific and nonspecific factors in psychotherapy: A problematic paradigm for psychotherapy research. *Psychotherapy, 23,* 30–40.

Cavenar Jr., J. O., & Brodie, H. K. H. (Eds.). (1983). *Signs and symptoms in psychiatry.* Philadelphia: Lippincott.

Chessick, R. D. (1993). The outpatient psychotherapy of the borderline patient. *American Journal of Psychotherapy, 47,* 206–227.

Clarkin, J. F., Marziali, E., & Munroe-Blum, H. (1991). Group and family treatments for borderline personality disorder. *Hospital and Community Psychiatry, 42,* 1038–1043.

Coale, H. E. (1992). Costume and pretend identities: A constructivist's use of experiences to co-create meanings with clients in therapy. *Journal of Strategic and Systemic Therapies, 11*(1), 45–55.

de Shazer, S. (1985). *Keys to solutions in brief therapy.* New York: Norton.

de Shazer, S. (1988). *Clues: Investigating solutions in brief therapy.* New York: Norton.

de Shazer, S. (1994). *Words were originally magic.* New York: Norton.

Duncan, B. L. (1992a). Strategic therapy, eclecticism, and the therapeutic relationship. *Journal of Marital and Family Therapy, 18,* 24–30.

Duncan, B. L. (1992b). Strategy and reality: A reply to Held, Goolishian, and Anderson. *Journal of Marital and Family Therapy, 18,* 39–40.

Duncan, B. L., & Moynihan, D. W. (1994). Applying outcome research: Intentional utilization of the client's frame of reference. *Psychotherapy, 31*(2), 294–302.

Duncan, B. L., Parks, M. B., & Rusk, G. S. (1990). Eclectic strategic practice: A process constructive perspective. *Journal of Marital and Family Therapy, 16,* 165–178.

Duncan, B. L., & Rock, J. W. (1991). *Overcoming relationship impasses: Ways to initiate change when your partner won't help.* New York: Insight.

Duncan, B. L., & Solovey, A. D. (1989). Strategic brief therapy: An insight-oriented approach? *Journal of Marital and Family Therapy, 15,* 1–9.

Duncan, B. L., Solovey, A. D., & Rusk, G. S. (1992). *Changing the rules: A client-directed approach to therapy.* New York: Guilford.

Dunn, G. E. (1992). Multiple personality disorder: A new challenge for psychology. *Professional Psychology: Research and Practice, 23,* 18–23.

Eisenbud, R. J. (1978). Countertransference: The therapist's turn on the couch. In G. D. Goldman & D. S. Milman (Eds.), *Psychoanalytic psychotherapy* (pp. 72–90). Reading, MA: Addison-Wesley.

Elkin, I., Shea, T., Watkins, J. T., Imber, S. D., Sotsky, S. M., Collins, I. F., Glass, D. R., Pilkonis, P. A., Leber, W. R., Dockerty, J. P., Fiester, S. J., & Parloff, M. B. (1989). National Institute of Mental Health treatment of depression collaborative research program: General effectivenes of treatments. *Archives of General Psychiatry, 46,* 971–982.

Everstine, D. S., & Everstine, L. (1983). *People in crisis: Strategic therapeutic interventions.* New York: Brunner/Mazel.

Erickson, M. H., & Rossi, E. L. (1979). *Hypnotherapy: An exploratory casebook.* New York: Irvington.

Fisch, R., Weakland, J., & Segal, L. (1982). *The tactics of change: Doing therapy briefly.* San Francisco: Jossey-Bass.

Flegenheimer, W. V. (1982). *Techniques of brief psychotherapy.* New York: Aronson.

Frances, A., Clarkin, J., & Perry, S. (1984). *Differential therapeutics in psychiatry: The art and science of treatment selection.* New York: Brunner/Mazel.

Frank, J. D., & Frank, J. B. (1991). *Persuasion and healing* (3rd ed.). Baltimore: Johns Hopkins.

Fraser, J. S. (1983). Paranoia: Interactional views on evolution and intervention. *Journal of Marital and Family Therapy, 9*(4), 383–391.

Garfield, S. L. (1989). *The practice of brief psychotherapy.* New York: Pergamon.

Garfield, S. L. (1978). Research on client variables in psychotherapy. In S. L. Garfield & A. E. Bergin (Eds.), *Handbook of psychotherapy and behavior change* (2nd ed., pp. 191–232). New York: Wiley.

Gaston, L. (1990). The concept of the alliance and its role in psychotherapy: Theoretical and empirical considerations. *Psychotherapy, 27,* 143–152.

Goolishian, H. A., & Anderson, H. (1987). Language systems and psychotherapy: An evolving idea. *Psychotherapy, 24,* 529–538.

Greening, T. (1996, August). *Can we help Humpty Dumpty—and can he help himself?* Paper presented at the annual meeting of the American Psychological association, Toronto.

Gunderson, J. G. (1989). Borderline personality disorder. In H. I. Kaplan & B. J. Sadock (Eds.), *Comprehensive textbook of psychiatry* (Vol. 2, 5th ed., pp. 1387–1395). Baltimore: Williams & Wilkins.

Gurman, A. S. (1977). Therapist and patient factors influencing the patient's perception of facilitative therapeutic conditions. *Psychiatry, 40,* 16–24.

Harding, C. M., Zubin, J., & Strauss, J. S. (1987). Chronicity in schizophrenia: Fact, partial fact or artifact. *Journal of Hospital and Community Psychiatry, 38,* 477–484.

Heath, A. W., & Atkinson, B. J. (1989). Solutions attempted and considered: Broadening assessment in brief therapy. *Journal of Strategic and Systemic Therapies, 8,* 56–57.

Held, B. S. (1986). The relationship between individual psychologies and strategic/systemic therapies reconsidered. In D. E. Efron (Ed.), *Journeys: Expansion of the strategic systemic therapies* (pp. 222–260). New York: Brunner/Mazel.

Held, B. S. (1991). The process/content distinction in psychotherapy revisited. *Psychotherapy, 28,* 207–217.

Hollon, S. D., & Beck, A. T. (1994). Cognitive and cognitive-behavioral therapies. In A. E. Bergin & S. L. Garfield (Eds.), *Handbook of psychotherapy and behavior change* (4th ed., pp. 428–466). New York: Wiley.

Horowitz, M., Marmar, C., Weiss, D., DeWitt, K., & Rosenbaum, R. (1984). Brief psychotherapy of bereavement reactions: The relationship of process to outcome. *Archives of General Psychiatry, 41,* 438–448.

Hoyt, M. F. (1994). On the importance of keeping it simple and taking the patient seriously: A conversation with Steve de Shazer and John Weakland. In M. F. Hoyt (Ed.), *Constructive therapies.* New York: Guilford.

Hubble, M. A., & O'Hanlon, W. H. (1992). Theory countertransference. *Dulwich Centre Newsletter,* (1), 25–30.

Hubble, M. A., & Solovey, A. D. (1994). Ambassadorship in medical rehabilitation: A remedy for noncompliance. *Journal of Systemic Therapies, 13*(3), 67–76.

Jacobson, N. S., & Addis, M. E. (1993). *Research on couple therapy: What do we know? Where are we going?* Unpublished manuscript.

Johnson, H. C. (1991). Borderline clients: Practice implications of recent research. *Social Work, 36,* 166–173.

Kaplan, H. I., Sadock, B. K., & Grebb, J. A. (1994). *Synopsis of Psychiatry* (7th ed.). Baltimore: William & Wilkins.

Kernberg, O., Selzer, M. A., Koenigsberg, H. W., Carr, A. C., & Appelbaum, A. H. (1987). *Psychodynamic psychotherapy of borderline patients.* New York: Basic.

Kluft, R. P. (1991a). Clinical presentations of multiple personality disorder. *Psychiatric Clinics of North America, 14,* 605–629.

Kluft, R. P. (1991b). Hospital treatment of multiple personality disorder: An overview. *Psychiatric Clinics of North America, 14,* 695–719.

Koerner, K., & Linehan, M. M. (1992). Integrative therapy for borderline personality: Dialectical behavior therapy. In J. C. Norcross & M. R. Goldfried (Eds.), *Handbook of psychotherapy integration* (pp. 433–459). New York: Basic.

Kopp, S. B. (1977). *Back to one: A practical guide for psychotherapists.* Palo Alto: Science and Behavior.

Koss, M. P., & Butcher, J. N. (1986). Research on brief psychotherapy. In S. L. Garfield & A. E. Bergin (Eds.), *Handbook of psychotherapy and behavior change* (3rd ed., pp. 627–670). New York: Wiley.

Koss, M. P., & Shiang, J. (1994). Research on brief psychotherapy. In A. E. Bergin & S. L. Garfield (Eds.), *Handbook of psychotherapy and behavior change* (4th ed., pp. 664–700). New York: Wiley.

Lafferty, P., Beutler, L. E., & Crago, M. (1989). Differences between more and less effective psychotherapists: A study of selected therapist variables. *Journal of Consulting and Clinical Psychology, 57,* 76–80.

Lambert, M. J. (1992). Implications of outcome research for psychotherapy integration. In J. C. Norcross & M. R. Goldfried (Eds.), *Handbook of psychotherapy integration* (pp. 94–129). New York: Basic.

Lambert M. J., & Bergin, A. E. (1994). The effectiveness of psychotherapy. In A. E. Bergin & S. L. Garfield (Eds.), *Handbook of psychotherapy and behavior change* (4th ed., pp. 143–189). New York: Wiley.

Lambert, M. J., Shapiro, D. A., & Bergin, A. E. (1986). The effectiveness of psychotherapy. In S. L. Garfield & A. E. Bergin (Eds.), *Handbook of psychotherapy and behavior change* (3rd ed., pp. 157–212). New York: Wiley.

Lowenstein, R. J. (1992). Multiple personality and psychoanalysis: An introduction. *Psychoanalytic Inquiry, 12,* 3–48.

Luborsky, L., Singer, B., & Luborsky, L. (1975). Comparative studies of psychotherapies: Is it true that "everybody has won and all must have prizes?" *Archives of General Psychiatry, 32,* 995–1008.

Manschreck, T. C. (1989). Delusional (paranoid) disorders. In H. I. Kaplan & B. J. Sadock (Eds.), *Comprehensive textbook of psychiatry* (Vol. 1, 5th ed., pp. 816–829). Baltimore: Williams & Wilkins.

Marmar, C., Horowitz, M., Weiss, D., & Marziali, E. (1986). The development of the Therapeutic Alliance Rating System. In L. Greenberg & W. Pinsof (Eds.), *The psychotherapeutic process: A research handbook* (pp. 367–390). New York: Guilford.

Meyer, R. G., & Salmon, P. (1988). *Abnormal psychology* (2nd ed.). Boston: Allyn & Bacon.

Miller, S. D. (1994). The solution conspiracy: A mystery in three installments. *Journal of Systemic Therapies, 13*(1), 18–37.

Miller, S. D., Duncan, B. L., & Hubble, M. A. (1997). *Escape from Babel: Toward a unifying language for psychotherapy practice.* New York: Norton.

Miller, S. D., Hubble, M. A., & Duncan, B. L. (Eds.). (1996). *Handbook of solution-focused brief therapy.* San Francisco: Jossey-Bass.

Murphy, P. M., Cramer, D., & Lillie, F. J. (1984). The relationship between curative factors perceived by patients in their psychotherapy and treatment outcome: An exploratory study. *British Journal of Medical Psychology, 57,* 187–192.

Nash, J. L. (1983). Delusions. In J. O. Cavenar, Jr. & H. K. H. Brodie (Eds.), *Signs and symptoms in psychiatry* (pp. 455–481). Philadelphia: Lippincott.

Nemiah, J. C. (1989). Dissociative disorders (hysterical neuroses, dissociative type). In H. I. Kaplan & B. J. Sadock (Eds.), *Comprehensive textbook of psychiatry* (Vol. 1, 5th ed., pp. 1028–1044). Baltimore: Williams & Wilkins.

Nyland, D., & Corsiglia, V. (1994). Becoming solution-focused forced in brief therapy: Remembering something important we already knew. *Journal of Systemic Therapies, 13*(1), 5–12.

O'Hanlon, W. (1990). A grand unified theory for brief therapy: Putting problems in context. In J. K. Zeig & S. G. Gilligan (Eds.), *Brief therapy: Myths, methods, and metaphors* (pp. 78–89). New York: Brunner/Mazel.

Orlinsky, D. E., & Howard, K. I. (1986). Process and outcome in psychotherapy. In S. L. Garfield & A. E. Bergin (Eds.), *Handbook of psychotherapy and behavior change* (3rd ed., pp. 311–381). New York: Wiley.

Orlinsky, D. E., Graw, K., & Parks, B. K. (1994). Process and outcome in psychotherapy—Noch Einmal. In A. E. Bergin & S. L. Garfield (Eds.), *Handbook of psychotherapy and behavior change* (4th ed., pp. 270–376). New York: Wiley.

Parry, A. (1991). A universe of stories. *Family Process, 30,* 37–54.

Patterson, C. H. (1984). Empathy, warmth, and genuineness in psychotherapy: A review of reviews. *Psychotherapy, 21,* 431–438.

Rogers, C. R. (1957). The necessary and sufficient conditions of therapeutic personality change. *Journal of Consulting Psychology, 21,* 95–103.

Rosenberg, R. (1994). Borderline states: Pharmacotherapy and psychobiology of personality: A discussion of Soloff's article. *Acta Psychiatrica Scandinavica,* (Suppl. 379), 56–60.

Rosenfield, I. (1988). *The invention of memory.* New York: Basic.

Rosenhan, D. L. (1973). On being sane in insane places. *Science, 179,* 250–258.

Salovey, P., & Turk, D. C. (1991). Clinical judgment and decision-making. In C. R. Snyder & D. R. Forsyth (Eds.), *Handbook of social and clinical psychology: The health perspective* (pp. 416–437). New York: Pergamon.

Shea, M. T. (1991). Standardized approaches to individual psychotherapy of patients with borderline disorder. *Hospital and Community Psychiatry, 42,* 1034–1038.

Shea, S. C. (1988). *Psychiatric interviewing: The art of understanding.* Philadelphia: Saunders.

Sloane, R. B., Staples, F. R., Cristol, A. H., Yorkston, N. J., & Whipple, K. (1975). *Psychotherapy versus behavior therapy.* Cambridge, MA: Harvard University Press.

Soloff, P. H. (1994). Is there any drug treatment of choice for the borderline patient? *Acta Psychiatrica Scandinavica,* (Suppl. 379), 50–55.

Smith, M. L., Glass, G. U., & Miller, T. J. (1980). *The benefits of psychotherapy.* Baltimore: Johns Hopkins University.

Temerlin, M. K. (1968). Suggestion effects in psychiatric diagnosis. *Journal of Nervous and Mental Disease, 147,* 349–353.

Walker, J. I., & Cavenar, Jr., J. O. (1983). Paranoid symptoms and conditions. In J. O. Cavenar, Jr. & H. K. H. Brodie (Eds.), *Signs and symptoms in psychiatry* (pp. 483–510). Philadelphia: Lippincott.

Watzlawick, P., Weakland, J., & Fisch, R. (1974). *Change: Problem formation and problem resolution.* New York: Norton.

Weakland, J. H., Fisch, R., Watzlawick, P., & Bodin, A. (1974). Brief therapy: Focused problem resolution. *Family Process, 13,* 141–168.

Webster's collegiate dictionary (10th ed.). (1993). New York: Merriam Webster.

Weinberger, J. (1995). Common factors aren't so common: The common factors dilemma. *Clinical Psychology: Science and Practice, 2,* 45–69.

Weiner, R. D. (1983). Amnesia. In J. O. Cavenar, Jr. & H. K. H. Brodie (Eds.), *Signs and symptoms in psychiatry* (pp. 575–596). Philadelphia: Lippincott.

Wright, B. A. (1991) Labeling: The need for greater person-environment individuation. In C. R. Snyder & D. R. Forsyth (Eds.), *Handbook of social and clinical psychology: The health perspective* (pp. 469–487). New York: Pergamon.

Zeig, J. K., & Gilligan, S. G. (Eds.). (1990). *Brief therapy: Myths, methods, and metaphors.* New York: Brunner/Mazel.

Zetzel, E. R. (1971). A developmental approach to the borderline patient. *American Journal of Psychiatry, 127,* 867–871.

INDEX

accommodation, 20, 22–34
  of client's resources, 23–26, 28, 51, 52–53
  of client's theory of change, x, 19–20, 31–32, 51, 60–65
  defined, 23
  summary and conclusions for, 34
  therapeutic process involved in, 23
  of therapeutic relationship, 26–31, 51, 54–55, 125–27
  utilization vs., 25
accountability, professional, ix, 3
Addis, M. E., 206
Aesop, 11
affirmation, defined, 66
agree and exaggerate strategy, 62, 63, 67
alcohol, in Eileen and Richard case, 192, 195
Aldrich, C. K., 8
Alexander, L. B., 32
Alice case (delusional disorder), 122, 124–53, 207
  client participation in, 133–34
  creativity in, 130–31
  family background in, 126, 137–41
  gambling metaphor in, 129, 130
  goals in, 125
  language of collaboration in, 131
  money question in, 127, 128, 132, 137, 139–40, 142, 144–46
  pathway to impossibility in, 130
  personal empowerment in, 142
  prior negative therapy experience in, 126, 127, 130
  saving face in, 135, 148
  solution in, 143–52
  theory of change in, 131, 135–36, 141–42, 153

therapeutic relationship in, 125–31, 138–39
  validation in, 127–30, 148, 152–53
  see also David
alters (entities), 74–88, 92–121
  access process for, 79, 80, 81, 85
  breaking down of, 74–75, 76, 78, 79, 80, 85, 88, 97
  description of, 76–77
  integration of, 115–16, 118–21
  retreat of, 88, 94, 96, 98
  return of access to, 105, 106
ambivalence, in close relationships, 5–6
American Psychiatric Association, 69, 155
amorous paranoia, 123
  see also Alice case
Anderson, H., 50
antidepressants, 30
anxiety
  of client, 12–13, 14, 66, 93, 137–39, 195–96, 203
  of David, 131–36
  dissociative identity disorder and, 93
  of Richard, 195–96
  separation, 12–13, 14
  of therapist, 38, 40, 41, 42, 73, 93, 173, 196
Appelbaum, A., 156
Ardrey, Robert, 122
Arkowitz, H., 27
Atkinson, B. J., 61
attention, therapist's maintaining of, 40
attribution effects (attribution creep)
  avoiding, 43–45, 75, 82
  in Jay case, 159
  in Natalie case, 73, 75, 82, 111
  as pathway to impossibility, 4–6, 12, 13–14, 73, 75, 82
authority, 47